W9-BBW-935

# IP TELEPHONY UNVEILED

### Kevin Brown

## Cisco Press

800 East 96th Street
Indianapolis, Indiana 46240 USA

# IP Telephony Unveiled

Kevin Brown

Copyright© 2004 Cisco Systems, Inc.

Published by:

Cisco Press

800 East 96th Street

Indianapolis, IN 46240 USA

Printed in the United States of America   5 6 7 8 9 0

Fifth Printing  May 2005

Library of Congress Cataloging-in-Publication Number: 2002114471

ISBN: 1-58720-075-9

## Trademark Acknowledgments

All terms mentioned in this book that are known to be trademarks or service marks have been appropriately capitalized. Cisco Press or Cisco Systems, Inc. cannot attest to the accuracy of this information. Use of a term in this book should not be regarded as affecting the validity of any trademark or service mark.

## Warning and Disclaimer

This book is designed to provide information about IP telephony. Every effort has been made to make this book as complete and as accurate as possible, but no warranty or fitness is implied.

The information is provided on an "as is" basis. The author, Cisco Press, and Cisco Systems, Inc. shall have neither liability nor responsibility to any person or entity with respect to any loss or damages arising from the information contained in this book or from the use of the discs or programs that may accompany it.

The opinions expressed in this book belong to the author and are not necessarily those of Cisco Systems, Inc.

## Feedback Information

At Cisco Press, our goal is to create in-depth technical books of the highest quality and value. Each book is crafted with care and precision, undergoing rigorous development that involves the unique expertise of members from the professional technical community.

Reader feedback is a natural continuation of this process. If you have any comments regarding how we could improve the quality of this book, or otherwise alter it to better suit your needs, you can contact us through e-mail at feedback@ciscopress.com. Please make sure to include the book title and ISBN in your message.

We greatly appreciate your assistance.

## Corporate and Government Sales

Cisco Press offers excellent discounts on this book when ordered in quantity for bulk purchases or special sales.

For more information, please contact:

**U.S. Corporate and Government Sales** 1-800-382-3419 corpsales@pearsontechgroup.com

For sales outside of the U.S. please contact:

**International Sales** 1-317-581-3793 international@pearsontechgroup.com

**Publisher**   John Wait

**Editor-in-Chief**   John Kane

**Cisco Representative**   Anthony Wolfenden

**Cisco Press Program Manager**   Nannette M. Noble

**Production Manager**   Patrick Kanouse

**Development Editor**   Jennifer Foster

**Senior Project Editor**   Sheri Cain

**Copy Editor**   Marianne Madeiros

**Technical Editors**   Mark Gallo, David Lovell, Anne Smith

**Editorial Assistant**   Tammi Barnett

**Cover and Book Designer**   Louisa Adair

**Composition**   Mark Shirar

**Indexer**   Tim Wright

CISCO SYSTEMS

**Corporate Headquarters**
Cisco Systems, Inc.
170 West Tasman Drive
San Jose, CA 95134-1706
USA
www.cisco.com
Tel:  408 526-4000
      800 553-NETS (6387)
Fax: 408 526-4100

**European Headquarters**
Cisco Systems International BV
Haarlerbergpark
Haarlerbergweg 13-19
1101 CH Amsterdam
The Netherlands
www-europe.cisco.com
Tel:  31 0 20 357 1000
Fax: 31 0 20 357 1100

**Americas Headquarters**
Cisco Systems, Inc.
170 West Tasman Drive
San Jose, CA 95134-1706
USA
www.cisco.com
Tel:  408 526-7660
Fax: 408 527-0883

**Asia Pacific Headquarters**
Cisco Systems, Inc.
Capital Tower
168 Robinson Road
#22-01 to #29-01
Singapore 068912
www.cisco.com
Tel: +65 6317 7777
Fax: +65 6317 7799

Cisco Systems has more than 200 offices in the following countries and regions. Addresses, phone numbers, and fax numbers are listed on the
**Cisco.com Web site at www.cisco.com/go/offices.**

Argentina • Australia • Austria • Belgium • Brazil • Bulgaria • Canada • Chile • China PRC • Colombia • Costa Rica • Croatia • Czech Republic
Denmark • Dubai, UAE • Finland • France • Germany • Greece • Hong Kong SAR • Hungary • India • Indonesia • Ireland • Israel • Italy
Japan • Korea • Luxembourg • Malaysia • Mexico • The Netherlands • New Zealand • Norway • Peru • Philippines • Poland • Portugal
Puerto Rico • Romania • Russia • Saudi Arabia • Scotland • Singapore • Slovakia • Slovenia • South Africa • Spain • Sweden
Switzerland • Taiwan • Thailand • Turkey • Ukraine • United Kingdom • United States • Venezuela • Vietnam • Zimbabwe

# About the Author

**Kevin Brown** is currently Vice President of the Convergence Development Group, a business within Norstan Inc., that develops convergence applications. Kevin has more than 20 years of experience in the voice and data telecommunications industry, and has held positions with technology pioneers such as IBM, ROLM, VMX, and Xerox. Kevin was vice president of sales and marketing for Selsius Systems at the time of the acquisition of Selsius Systems by Cisco Systems. He spent three and a half years in the Enterprise Voice Video Business Unit at Cisco Systems prior to accepting his current position at Norstan. Today, he leads a team of application developers and channel managers who design, develop, and deploy convergence applications for medium-size and enterprise clients. Kevin speaks at various corporate and company functions, and has a wife, Georgina, and six children.

# About the Technical Reviewers

**Mark Gallo** is a technical manager with America Online, where he leads a group of engineers responsible for the design and deployment of the domestic corporate intranet. His network certifications include Cisco CCNP and Cisco CCDP. He has led several engineering groups responsible for designing and implementing enterprise LANs and international IP networks. He has a BS in electrical engineering from the University of Pittsburgh. Mark resides in northern Virginia with his wife, Betsy, and son, Paul.

**David Lovell** is an educational specialist at Cisco Systems, Inc., where he designs, develops, and delivers training on CIPT networks. David is experienced in design and implementation of IP telephony systems and has been instructing students for eight years, four of which have focused solely on IP telephony.

**Anne Smith** is a technical writer in the CallManager engineering group at Cisco Systems. She has written technical documentation for the Cisco IP Telephony solution since CallManager release 2.0 and was part of the Selsius Systems acquisition in 1998. Anne writes internal and external documents for CallManager, IP phones, and other Cisco IP Telephony products. She is a co-author of *Cisco CallManager Fundamentals* (ISBN: 1-58705-008-0), *Developing Cisco IP Phone Services* (ISBN: 1-58705-060-9), and *Troubleshooting Cisco IP Telephony* (ISBN: 1-58705-075-7), all from Cisco Press.

# Dedications

I dedicate this book to a number of people from my personal and professional life. First of all, to my wife Georgina, and our children: Tylen, Alex, Colin, Matt, Mikey, and Madalyn—who always remind me of who I am. To my parents for being who they are.

On the professional front, thanks to David Tucker (co-founder of Selsius Systems, now with Cisco Systems), my professional mentor; Pat Howard (formerly with VMX and now with QuantumShift), who remains, in my mind, a visionary of the highest order; and Cari c'deBaca, who in the convergence industry, "gets it" and "articulates it" better than anyone I know.

# Acknowledgments

IP telephony has come a long way in a short period of time thanks to a number of people, many of whom have either directly contributed to, or influenced this writing. First and foremost, thanks to David Tucker for bringing me into this industry and for entrusting so much to me. Thanks to Cari c'deBaca for being someone who, to this day, remains my sounding board for ideas and strategies. Thanks to Steve Foster for his contributions and ideas during the hardest of circumstances. Thanks to Toni Baych, of Vertex Consulting Group, for her expertise in always reminding me to make this relevant to the customer, not the technology itself, and to Ken Bywaters (from Berbee Communications) and Alok Jain (formerly of NetCom Systems, now with Norstan), two of the initial pioneers in the IPT application development practice. Finally, thanks to Mick Buchanan and David Lovell, two of the strongest technical advisers I know in this industry.

# Contents at a Glance

# Contents

# Icons Used in This Book

Network Device Icons

CallManager

IP Phone

Stations

SRST Router

Used For:
Application Server
DHCP
DNS
MOH Server
MTP
SW Conference Bridge
Voice Mail Server

Router

Switch

Layer 3 Switch

PIX Firewall

Gateway or
3rd-Party
H.323
Server

Modem

Access Server

ATM Switch

Used For:
Analog Gateway
Gatekeeper
Gateway
H.323 Gateway
Voice-Enabled Router

PBX/PSTN Switch

PBX (Small)

Cisco
Directory
Server

Local Director

PC

Laptop

Server

PC w/Software

Used For:
HW Conference Bridge
Transcoder
Voice-Enabled Switch

POTS Phone

Relational
Database

Fax Machine

---

Media/Building Icons

Network Cloud

Ethernet Connection

Serial Connection

Telecommuter

Building

Branch
Office

# Introduction

To some, IP telephony (IPT) is the next step in the evolution of voice technologies. In reality, it is far more than that. IP telephony redefines the role voice plays in the enterprise business environment. Placing voice on the IP network goes beyond placing phone calls—although that is important. However, at the desktop level, IPT means new clients, new applications, and new services.

Since early 2002, there has been an explosion of new applications, the scope and vision of which were not even imagined by the vendors launching the products just one year prior. For manufacturers and their channels of distribution, this means a new revenue and support model. For customers, it means new opportunities to impact their businesses in ways heretofore unimagined.

Companies today are looking for initiatives to help them generate more revenue, make the revenue they have more profitable, and satisfy their customers in the hopes of building customer loyalty. The current economic downturn has not changed these objectives. Rather, it has placed them front and center in the minds of senior management, and IP telephony, when properly understood and implemented, becomes a key enabler for their key business initiatives.

The challenge is that IP telephony, as a component of a convergence strategy, is one of the fastest emerging markets in the telecommunications space, and yet it is also filled with misunderstandings and misinformation. When one person talks about IP telephony, he or she might envision something entirely different than what another person envisions. Therefore, "why" a customer chooses to converge is often more important than "how" a customer chooses to converge. Ultimately, the partner they select to travel on this journey with them might be the most important choice they make. IP telephony can absolutely impact a customer's business model in tremendous ways. IPT can open new revenue streams, enhance profitability, drive new levels of customer and employee satisfaction, and it can be a key enabler in a company's strategy to differentiate itself competitively. Yet, it can only do these things if that is part of the desired goal. All too often, customers see IPT only as a "new telephone system" and, therefore, they remain unaware of the strategic enabler laying dormant in their business.

This book awakens senior managers to the real benefits of an IP telephony strategy, and provides assistance in developing this strategy inside their own organizations.

For the readers of this book, I hope you come away with four key elements:

- Understand the difference between VoIP and IP telephony, and what that means for your business. This is critical, because many people incorrectly use these two terms interchangeably.

- Understand that this is not new, unproven technology. This book illustrates that thousands of customers have already implemented the technology.

- A realistic expectation for ROI. Many companies become so fixated on the perceived savings they believe they should be receiving that they begin to make strategic mistakes. IP telephony might initially involve a considerable cost. It is the business impact and the post-install process improvements that give you the much anticipated payback.

- Recognize potential business-impacting applications within your own organization.

With that, sit back—and enjoy!

# CHAPTER 1

# HAVEN'T WE BEEN HERE BEFORE?

It's the spring of 1998. I'm having lunch with two old friends, David Tucker and Richard Platt, at an Outback Steakhouse restaurant. We are discussing the company they have cofounded, Selsius Systems. They tell me that they have developed the perfect technology for the integration of voice, data, and video. Thinking back on that lunch meeting now, I remember stirring my iced tea with a sense of déjà vu. My mind immediately wanders back to 1986.

In 1986, while working for ROLM Corporation, I was part of a team that sold and installed a voice and data integration solution to a large university in Dallas, Texas. David Tucker was the sales manager leading the team. We installed over a thousand digital telephones with data connectivity to allow the connection of asynchronous devices to the ROLM CBX selected by the university.

One of the key criteria for the university was their desire for a more cost-effective means of connecting data devices to various data sources, both internal and external. They looked at the PBX as the logical staging point for integrating voice and data. They bought into the promise of easier administration, of single wiring to the desktop, of shared access to various data hosts—all in the name of saving dollars.

Years later, in 1994, David and I were together again, this time at Intecom, where we continued to blur the lines between voice and data with a product called InteLAN. InteLAN was a connectivity hub integrated into the Intecom PBX and was the brainchild of an engineering team headed by Richard Platt.

Fast forward to the Outback Steakhouse in 1998. I am listening to David and Richard excitedly discuss this new product and where it is going to take the industry. I remember the single, simple thought that jumped into my head at that moment:

"Haven't we been down this road before?"

I suspect that many people, when they first hear of IP telephony (IPT), react in much the same manner.

"Here we go again."

"Voice and Data Integration, Part 2."

I can't blame people for thinking this, because in many aspects, it is true. Integrating voice and data into a single platform is not a new idea. (Some might argue it is not even a *good* idea, but I'll cover that later.) The PBX manufacturers championed this concept back in the 1980s. The idea at that time was to use the PBX and voice infrastructure as the focal point for integrating the two technologies. In many respects, this made perfect sense, primarily because of the high reliability perceptions of the PBX and voice infrastructure.

This chapter explains why a PBX, despite its high reliability, is not a solution for convergence. It also examines what makes IPT different from earlier approaches to convergence, and discusses application development as the key to successful IPT deployment.

# The PBX as a Convergence Platform

The PBX is arguably the most reliable technology mankind has created and so it seems a logical choice to use as the platform for integration. If you talk to most people, the perception they have is that although their mainframe might hiccup and their network might snooze every now and then, the telephone system is the one constant, the "old reliable." It doesn't break and it is always available. You pick up a phone, and you hear dial tone. It just works. So, with that in mind, in the 1980s, if you were going to bring voice and data together, the PBX, with its high reliability, was a natural starting point.

Figure 1-1 offers an accurate view of voice and data integration as it was implemented in 1986. For those users who chose this solution, a single drop of wiring to the desktop was sufficient to handle both voice and data sessions. Many manufacturers offered the capability to connect voice and data desktop devices to the PBX, and of course, Integrated Services Digital Network (ISDN) Basic Rate Interface (BRI)—the basic rate interface with two information channels and a signaling channel (2B+D)—gave the industry an attempt at a standards-based way of delivering voice and data services to the desktop.

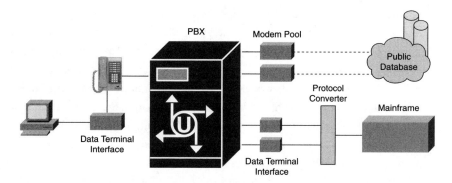

***Figure 1-1*** *PBX Voice/Data Integration in the Mid-1980s*

In Figure 1-1, the PC attaches to the telephone by means of a data terminal interface. PBX manufacturers had different names for this device. It was often called a datacom module, or a voice-data integration module, among other things. Regardless of the terminology used, this unit had a single function: convert the asynchronous stream of data into a format suitable for transport within either a single or dual timeslot. This device was found on both the upstream and downstream links; that is, at the desktop and at the host or computer location. In this manner, data devices were connected to the PBX and used the PBX as a means of connecting to a host computer, and shared the same wire as the phone connected to the PBX, resulting in cost savings.

So, on the surface, it looks like there was a solution almost 20 years ago for the "voice and data" industry. The solution worked as advertised, in terms of functionality and ease of use. It certainly introduced new desktop devices to the industry—such as the Cypress voice/data workstation and Cedar voice/data PC offerings from ROLM—and in many cases, was a cost-effective alternative to hard-wired data devices. However, this approach did have some drawbacks:

- It was contention-based.

- It lacked industry standards.

- PBX architecture provided insufficient connection rates.

## Contention

The concept of pooling, or contention, was a key component of the PBX-based voice and data strategy. Contention-based connectivity was both a benefit and a detriment to the convergence strategy in the 1980s. A contention-based solution allowed companies to deploy fewer ports to the host computers than users. In other words, there could be potentially hundreds or thousands of users contending for a limited number of ports. If a port was not available, then users were not granted access to the host computer. This was often the case with PCs or asynchronous terminals running some type of 3270 emulation package for access to an IBM (or compatible) mainframe. It was not uncommon to see a protocol converter emulate an IBM 3270 cluster.

The protocol converter, as shown in Figure 1-2, while hard-wired to the host computer, allowed PBX-connected devices to "pool" or contend for incoming ports. When all ports were filled, the users either automatically rolled to ports associated with the next protocol converter defined to the PBX (if available) or received a busy tone.

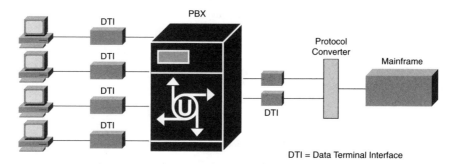

**Figure 1-2**  *A PBX Allowing Data Workstations to Contend for Limited Ports on a Protocol Converter*

In Figure 1-2, four asynchronous workstations (VT100, PCs in async mode) contend for two slots on a protocol converter. The protocol converter converts the asynchronous data stream into a suitable format, such as 3270 for IBM System 370 machines, for presentation to the host computer.

This approach had both benefits and drawbacks. The main benefit was that companies were able to deploy lower cost asynchronous terminals (typically VT-100 type) instead of the more expensive 3278/3279/3179 devices. For users with personal computers, using less expensive asynchronous emulation cards instead of expensive 3270 emulator cards helped lower the costs to the organization. Also, because contention did not provide dedicated ports for every user, fewer "cluster controllers" were needed (protocol converters in this case) for direct access to the host environment.

The drawbacks, however, outweighed the benefits for many organizations. Because the goal was cost savings, as previously noted, each user did not have a dedicated port. For those users who only occasionally needed access to the host computers, this was a fairly decent solution. Yet, for those users who were accustomed to having access whenever they needed it, getting a busy signal was totally unacceptable. Here was a case where the traditional telephony way of handling a scenario (giving a user a busy signal) was, for some data users, out of the question.

## Lack of Industry Standards

Another problem data users encountered with the PBX was a lack of standards. In the data world, it was necessary to adhere to certain standards. When connecting to a host, the Information Systems (IS) staff had to decide what kind of terminal to emulate, or imitate. So it was common knowledge among IS and telecom people that they might have to emulate a 3270 environment, a 5250 environment, a VT-100 environment, or an HP or Data General or Wang environment, and there were packages that enabled each and any of these emulations.

Utilizing the PBX, however, consideration had to be given to the type of port connectivity for desktop and host devices. Because of the lack of standards, the devices manufactured by one company weren't necessarily the same as the devices manufactured by other companies. So the data terminal interfaces that each vendor used were different, and each data manufacturer had to test against each PBX manufacturer without the benefits of standards.

## Insufficient Connection Rate

However, more than anything else, the real issue companies faced trying to satisfy their data users when integrating into the PBX was the connection rate (line speed). Users who previously were accustomed to host-connected, or channel speeds (often in the 1–2 Mbps range), were now throttled down between 64–128 kpbs, which was the maximum connection rate that a PBX allowed. The reason for this was that a PBX allocated bandwidth in the form of timeslots, and each timeslot was, by definition, 64 kbps. This was the standard connection for voice. By providing two timeslots, data users were allowed double that connectivity.

For the "casual user" (a term created by the industry), this was generally acceptable. However, many users resisted the term. "There's nothing casual about my work requirements," they reasoned, insisting that their connectivity, although not continuous, was just as important and urgent. In the end, the slower speeds (which meant users watching their screens get "painted" line by line) and the busy signals doomed this approach. Contention and low connect speeds doomed voice-data integration in the 1980s. IP telephony eliminates these obstacles to convergence. Certainly, if IPT is going to work, it has to address the issues that grounded the movement to a halt in the early 1980s.

# The IPT Difference

During that fateful lunch with David and Richard, I kept wondering why IP telephony was so different. More than that, I wondered why two men that I knew and respected were so excited about it. The answer was brilliant in its simplicity. In their minds, the problem with the efforts to integrate voice and data in the 1980s and early 1990s was not technical, but a matter of focus. Instead of trying to squeeze bandwidth-intensive data into PBX timeslots, the better answer might be to place voice, which needs little bandwidth, into a data network where bandwidth is generally more accessible.

This change in focus provides the premise for the remainder of the issues discussed throughout this book: IP telephony, properly understood and deployed, can help organizations realize numerous benefits that they might not be considering today. At the center of these benefits are applications—new world applications—that transcend the traditional boundaries placed between voice and data environments.

## Voice over IP

Voice over IP (VoIP) is exactly what it appears to be: deploying voice over an IP network. In its most basic form, VoIP means placing voice traffic onto the IP network for transport purposes only. Many people in the industry today who adopt this view of VoIP refer to the IP network as "plumbing"; i.e., the network is the plumbing (pipes) used to carry information (in this case, voice). Figure 1-3 shows an example of VoIP, according to this basic definition.

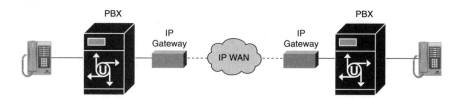

***Figure 1-3*** *VoIP: Users from Two PBXs "Talk" Across the IP Network, Thus Saving Long-Distance Charges*

Figure 1-3 illustrates how an IP gateway (often referred to as an IP blade) that is added to the existing PBX gives those PBX users the ability to place calls over a company's IP network from location to location in order to reduce long-distance charges. Toll-bypass, as this is commonly referred to, is the most obvious benefit of this type of VoIP deployment.

In Figure 1-3, the IP gateway could easily be a single card that is installed/integrated into the PBX as are other cards on a PBX shelf. Furthermore, it could be a card within a data router that currently resides on a company's IP network. Either approach (integrated as a card in the PBX or a router) provides organizations with a cost-effective means for integrating gateways into their environments. For many companies, reducing long-distance charges has been the desired state, and upon accomplishing this task, they move on to other projects. In their minds, their VoIP project is completed.

## The Telephone as Client

Many organizations, however, see VoIP as far more than this. More than simply using the network as transport (or plumbing), many organizations see value in not only placing voice "traffic" onto the IP network, but also in placing the actual voice "clients" (the telephones themselves) and new voice applications onto the IP network. This approach, although technically still VoIP, is commonly referred to as *IP telephony*; i.e., deploying a total telephony solution (including telephones, components, applications, and by extension, users) within the IP network.

In other words, IPT takes the premise of voice and data integration to its natural, albeit long-awaited conclusion: new voice clients (telephones, wireless devices, and desktop software) that, in their basic form, are designed to interface and interact with an IP network, obeying the rules of the IP network, utilizing its protocols, managed by its resources, and most importantly, accessing the myriad of applications that (can) exist on the network.

| NOTE | Whereas VoIP places voice traffic on the IP network, IP telephony places voice clients, applications, and traffic on the IP network, thereby providing a different value proposition. |
| --- | --- |

As shown in Figure 1-4, IP telephony allows phones to be directly connected to the IP network. A new type of phone, called an *IP phone*, is designed to interface directly to the Ethernet switch on the IP network, much like any other IP device, such as a PC, a laptop computer, or a network printer.

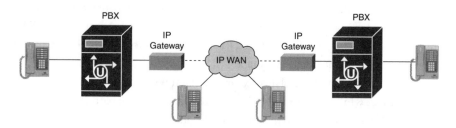

**Figure 1-4**  *IP Phones Connect Directly to the IP Network*

So, for the purpose of this book, VoIP is defined as technology that places voice traffic onto the IP network, whereas IP telephony is technology that places voice clients and voice applications as well as voice traffic onto the IP network. Each technology has a different goal, or desired state. The value proposition provided by IPT is very different than what was described previously for VoIP, primarily because the desired state for IP telephony is different.

The question most often asked by companies who investigate IP telephony is a simple one: Why should I put my telephones on the IP network? The simple answer is because managing one network instead of two (or more) is easier and more cost-effective, and that is where the majority of applications reside.

Unlike the traditional applications generally associated with voice, this new breed of applications is different. New applications are being developed quickly, with fewer resources, and at a lower cost. Instead of developing applications against a specific vendors' proprietary operating environment, IPT allows organizations to write applications using industry-standard (and widely used) data languages and protocols. In this new environment, just as data applications are written using Java, XML, HTML, Visual Basic or other similar tools, so too are new voice applications. Application development time is reduced from years and months to days and weeks. At Selsius Systems, we saw this trend develop in front of our eyes.

## Application Development: The Real Potential of IPT

The greatest benefit to be realized from IPT is in product development. A complex voice-mail application can be written, tested, productized, and delivered to the market in a short time period because of the standards-based environment of IP telephony. The standards-based environment of IP provides protocols and programming languages that are known to a large body of developers, worldwide. This means expanding the pool of talent to create applications beyond the ranks of a manufacturer, and into the entire market of LAN and workstation developers. An example of this occurred at Selsius Systems in October of 1998.

This time, while in a meeting with David Tucker and Richard Platt, we were joined by Dave Corley, who headed up Product Management. The topic of discussion was voice mail; specifically, our own. Up to this point, Selsius Systems, as a wholly owned subsidiary of Intecom Systems, enjoyed a fairly positive relationship with its parent company. However, over time, many Intecom employees began viewing the upstart Selsius organization as competitors and as a drain on their own financial resources. The more than 60 Selsius employees had their own Selsius IP phones on their desktops, but still used the Digital Sound voice-mail system used by Intecom employees. So, in this meeting, we discussed the need to have our own voice-messaging solution to further reduce our dependence on Intecom telecommunications resources.

During this meeting, we discussed our specific voice-mail requirements with Paul Clark, one of the Selsius developers. We knew we wanted this to be a software solution, one that did not depend on hardware ports (channels), and we knew we wanted the solution to be linked to our Microsoft Exchange e-mail environment. Paul Clark was the lone engineer assigned to the project. Not only were we asking Paul to develop a messaging environment for the employees of Selsius Systems, but also a messaging environment for our group to bring to the emerging IPT market as well.

So, in October of 1998, Paul Clark walked out of the meeting with his assignment. Less than two months later, the application was up and running, providing the voice-mail features we required, and linking to our Outlook application so that we could access our voice messages within Outlook and directly from phones.

This was an important milestone for me, because a few years before, I had worked as a senior product marketing manager with VMX, the founding organization of voice mail. In that capacity, I had the opportunity to see many development projects in action. So the notion of putting requirements in the hands of a single development engineer and actually having a product, working and being delivered to clients less than eight weeks later was not lost on me.

Looking back, I can honestly say that was the defining moment for me. Watching a complex voice-mail application be written, tested, productized, and delivered to the market in such a short amount of time convinced me that IPT was going to open a new frontier of application development similar to what is now seen with data-based Internet environments. All of us knew, at that point, that the application potential for IPT could truly be realized.

# Convergence: The Business Case for IPT

IP telephony is more than just reduced Moves, Adds, and Changes (MAC). It has become more than simplified or reduced cabling. It transcends reduced maintenance costs. All those are important, and they can help control costs. However, to truly appreciate the potential of IP telephony, telephones must be seen as new clients. Look past the handset and dialing pad, and envision a workstation running on the network and talking to applications—applications that are used to assist companies in running their day-to-day business operations. So the challenge facing businesses today as they look at IP telephony is to understand the technology in its capacity as a client. To do this, businesses need to ask key questions:

- How will deploying IPT bring about change in the way I do business?
- How will deploying IPT enable me to better control costs in my organization?
- How will deploying IPT enable me to more easily achieve the business objectives and corporate initiatives my company has in place?

These three questions represent the fork in the road for companies investigating IP telephony. Asking these questions raises the stakes considerably by forcing businesses to consider the impact that IPT will have on the company's operations, and on its budgets.

The early attempts to integrate voice and data in the 1980s certainly provided productivity gains. They also provided cost savings through simplified wiring, sharing of resources, and a reduction in the cost of data workstations. Yet these integration attempts did so at a cost most organizations found too steep (in response time and availability of host resources, as previously noted.) The point of any technology, and IP telephony in particular, is to enable companies to achieve business results, to impact business processes. As Maurice Ficklin, IS Manager at the University of Arkansas Pine Bluff notes, technology should level the playing field between companies, regardless of size and/or scope.

In this respect, IP telephony fits the bill. From the small company to the large enterprise, IPT can truly positively impact business process—if that is the desired goal of the company. Companies are looking for new ways to generate revenue, to control costs, to satisfy their customers and employees, to drive productivity, and to competitively differentiate themselves.

How IP telephony impacts these key initiatives in your organization is up to you—and your vision of this technology. You will find that based on your paradigm (an often overused word, but applicable here), IPT is either a new telephone system, or a network-based business model designed to drive change and improvement in your business processes.

Throughout the remainder of this book, I will elaborate on this key point, as I discuss the benefits that entice companies to converge, as well as the potential obstacles to convergence.

## Convergence as a Change Agent

Convergence will change many aspects of your organization. It will change how you deploy voice, data, and video solutions and also change how you view these technologies. Convergence will change how you manage these technologies in your environment, and how you organize yourself to take advantage of this new model. It will also change devices at the desktop, applications on the network, the expectations of reliability of the network, and the expectations that voice will have in your organization. In addition, it will facilitate change in the empowerment of desktop users when it comes to voice, and change how you cost-justify new technology solutions. Finally (and most importantly), convergence will bring about change in organizational responsibilities.

IP telephony might not be well received by the telecom engineer who sees the network engineer as somewhat of threat. Similarly, the network engineer might not be too enthusiastic about adapting to the different culture of supporting mission-critical voice communications. In the end, how comfortably your organization embraces change goes a long way in determining the success of an IPT deployment.

The best definition I have seen of convergence, as it relates to IP telephony, came from Cari c'deBaca, a product manager within the business unit at Cisco Systems responsible for their IPT solutions. "Convergence brings previously disparate networks together with the specific goal of impacting business in ways previously unimagined using applications previously not considered." Now, whereas this might sound like marketing fluff, in fact, it truly describes what I have witnessed in the past two years alone—new applications, developed by customers and third-party developers, that have redefined the role voice (and voice instruments) play in the enterprise.

Figure 1-5 is a screenshot of an actual application used at Cisco Systems in 2001. It was a Monday morning, just over a year after the Cisco Systems acquisition of Selsius Systems by which Cisco entered the IP telephony market. As employees of the business unit walked into their offices and cubes that morning, they saw this alert on their phones. This was an excellent way to let users know about the new voice-mail system, because it eliminated the need for lengthy print-out notices, e-mails, and training flyers—all which cost money. When users saw the notice, they were reminded of the new voice-mail system, and by depressing the "Details" soft button, they were given details on how to use the new system, thus eliminating expensive training program requirements. This is an example of new-world IPT applications in action, impacting business processes.

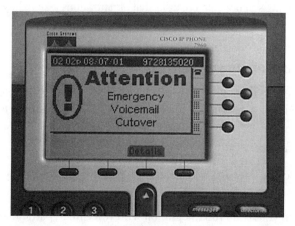

***Figure 1-5*** *IP Telephony Application Reminds Users of a New Voice-Mail System*

| NOTE | The true test of IP telephony is this: How has IP telephony changed the way your company conducts business? |
|------|---|

The bottom line: Convergence is all about change, and your organization might put up a fight against convergence. There are factions within every organization that inherently fight against change.

The manager responsible for mission-critical operations has been known to resist IP telephony for fear of introducing the unknown into the equation. In reality, this person cannot be blamed for resisting change because he will be held responsible for up-time and ongoing availability. Asking him to embrace and implement a new technology, such as IP telephony, is somewhat far-fetched (especially considering the horror stories proliferated by many publications regarding IPT in recent years).

Equally, the telecom manager has been known to resist IP telephony for fear of the abrupt end to a career. After all, it will mean IP clients and IP applications running on an IP network, obeying the rules of the IP network, managed by IP management platforms. What is overlooked here is that although these are indeed IP clients and applications, they are also voice clients and applications. If nothing else, the last three to four years have shown that the role of the telecom department becomes even more critical with IP telephony. Yet, on the surface, it does not seem so.

The end users, who have seen the same telephone on their desktop for likely the last decade, may certainly resist a new instrument unless new capabilities are introduced at the same time. Asking employees to learn how to use a new phone, and potentially a new voice messaging solution, are not tasks that organizations take lightly.

## Obstacles to Convergence

Additionally, technological obstacles might rear their heads against your convergence journey. I refer to these obstacles as "the usual suspects." They are predictable in nature and, with the proper planning, these issues can be anticipated and addressed easily:

- How do you interface your new IP telephony deployment to your existing legacy PBX environment?

- How do you retain full integration with voice mail, particularly message-waiting integration, if not all of your users migrate to IP telephony at the same time?

- How do you ensure that your IP network has the capacity to handle new voice users and their applications?

- When do you pilot the technology and, more importantly, what should be the purpose of a pilot?

- Are your processes for supporting the IP network consistent with the level of support your users are accustomed to receiving with their PBX phones?

- Have you identified all the features your users require?

- Have you identified new business-changing applications? If so, who is going to create them?

- Who supports the overall solution?

These are just a few of the questions that will be tackled in the following chapters. Rest assured, many of these issues are lurking in your organization. In fact, the one key that has been well proven in this industry is simply this: Don't rush into this technology without a plan. Develop a plan, execute the plan methodically, and avoid short-cuts. With proper planning and vision, the potential obstacles are easily overcome. Technology does not solve all problems. In fact, technology without a concrete blueprint for deployment can cause more problems than it solves.

Clearly, this sounds so obvious it almost should go without mention. Surprisingly, however, the majority of IP telephony installations that have had challenges were the results of poor planning rather than poor technology. Later chapters detail examples of this.

# Issues to Ponder

If convergence is about change, how is an IP telephony deployment going to change the way you conduct business? Change is often viewed from a negative perspective, but what if IP telephony could introduce positive change into your organization? How can IPT change the profitability of a business unit? How can it enhance customer satisfaction? How can you open new models of revenue generation with this technology? Isn't it true that the reason organizations deploy new technologies is to drive new efficiencies, which lead to business impact in critical areas? More than anything else, that is the goal of IP telephony.

As an enabler to a change strategy in your organization, this technology can drive new business productivity, change your profitability model, enhance existing business processes… or it can be a new telephone system. An organization's view of IPT will absolutely enhance, or limit, its impact on that organization.

# CHAPTER 2

# WAIT A MINUTE... MY PHONE SYSTEM WORKS JUST FINE...

The following scene has become familiar over the past few years since the acquisition of Selsius Systems by Cisco Systems in 1998: A customer comes to the Enterprise Voice, Video Business Unit (EVVBU) offices of Cisco in Dallas, Texas. He is interested in IP telephony and has come to see the technology in action. At this time, 200 IP phones are in the building. (A year later, when the business unit moves during a consolidation of buildings, that number increases to over 2500.) As with most of the 200-plus companies who visited the Dallas facility that year, this customer is pleasantly surprised to see this technology working well in a production environment.

Early in 2000, most articles written about IPT were cautious at best. The typical article might have discussed some of the potential benefits of IPT, but concluded with a myriad of reasons why the technology was not yet ready for full-time production deployment. Although many experts during this time acknowledged that IP telephony would be a common sight in organizations at some point, most agreed it was still a distant event.

So, clients who came into the EVVBU facility expecting only presentation slides and a demonstration environment were not prepared to also see hundreds of production users depending on this technology as their sole telephony solution. This clearly contradicted everything being written and said about this emerging technology. Furthermore, to learn that this new technology was every bit as reliable as the traditional PBX technology running in their current environments was also a surprising revelation.

"This technology works very well," someone invariably would say. As if on queue, someone in the customer organization (usually from the telecom department) would make the following observation: "So does our PBX."

That becomes the crux of the matter for many people looking at IP telephony: "My current telephone system works just fine."

If your phone system works fine as it is, why, indeed, would you look at a brand-new technology? Needing a new phone system and needing a new phone system that works differently than your current system are not the same thing. Usually, when phone systems become old, most people don't debate needing to replace their PBX, but they do debate buying a new one that runs on the IP network. Their concerns are usually based on valid points:

- The data network is unreliable.

- We've never had an outage with our PBX.

- My IP network was not designed for voice.

The last concern is mentioned most often, and is the focus of this chapter. Understanding how a network can be designed—from its inception—to handle voice and data, is a foundational requirement for those who hope to support IP telephony in their organizations.

# The PBX Environment

In a corporate telephony environment, there is a constant methodology for how voice technology works. As shown in Figure 2-1, a PBX is a self-contained environment designed to provide all the necessary features, functionality, and connectivity required within a cabinet (or series of cabinets). Within the cabinets of a traditional PBX are line cards, trunk cards, a CPU (possibly two, if redundancy is required), a TDM switching environment, and various card-sets that handle ringing, tone generation, dial tone, etc.

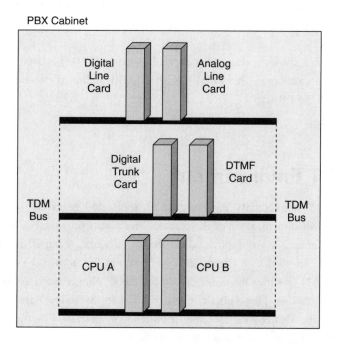

*Figure 2-1* *PBX Internal Workings, Including Shelves, Line Cards, Trunk Cards, and CPUs*

| NOTE | With IP telephony, each function from a PBX is replicated in some fashion on the IP network, through a combination of hardware, firmware, and software. |
| --- | --- |

In a traditional PBX environment, as shown in Figure 2-1, a look inside the chassis/main cabinet of a PBX reveals that the PBX is a TDM switching environment. Each voice session is assigned a timeslot, or a piece of bandwidth, for the duration of the session. The telephones connect (through a cable plan) to a line card on one of the PBX shelves. This line card can either be a digital card or an analog card, depending upon the type of telephone. The line card provides the hardware connectivity between the telephone and the PBX switching environment.

Additionally, external trunks (links) to the public switched telephone network (PSTN) allow external connectivity for incoming and outgoing calls (i.e., calls not initiated and terminated on an internal extension). Just as with the line cards, the trunk cards can either be analog or digital. Digital cards usually are T-1, E-1, or ISDN links.

Figure 2-1 shows a time-division multiplexing (TDM) bus connecting the shelves within a cabinet. This TDM bus is the highway that allows information to travel within the PBX.

# The IPT Environment

The PBX connectivity environment is replicated precisely in a pure IP telephony environment. Each of the connectivity points previously discussed and shown in Figure 2-1 are duplicated on the IP network, using IP infrastructure components. As shown in Figure 2-2, an Ethernet (or network) switch on the corporate LAN provides the connectivity for the IP clients, such as desktop and laptop workstations. These clients (also referred to as devices) are designed to interface to the IP network by using a built-in or modular Ethernet adapter to connect to the network switch on the network.

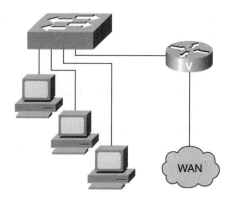

***Figure 2-2*** *Desktop Connectivity for IP Workstations*

In Figure 2-2, each device has a corresponding port on the network switch; that is, each of the desktop workstations and laptops has an associated network switch port for connectivity into the IP network. This holds true for the network router shown for intersite IP communications and network printers (not shown).

In Figure 2-3, IP phone connectivity into the IP network, the network switch duplicates the functionality of the line card in a traditional PBX environment. In other words, the network switch replaces the line card for desktop telephone connectivity. In a pure IP telephony environment, an IP phone is designed to interface with a network switch port in its native form, just like other traditional IP clients. A true IP phone uses established IP network protocols for communication sessions, and interfaces with the network cabling plan using an RJ-45 connection.

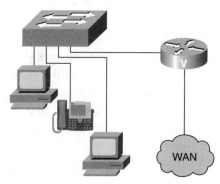

***Figure 2-3*** *IP Phone Connectivity into the IP Network*

Figure 2-3 shows how the IP phone and the IP workstation (whether a desktop or a laptop) both use the same type of port on the network switch (i.e., an Ethernet port that is designed to interface with both data and voice clients at the desktop).

Similarly, just as the functionality of the telephony line card is duplicated in the network switch for IP phone connectivity, the functionality for accessing the PSTN through analog and/or digital trunks must also be replicated. The IP telephony model does this by use of gateways. In the strictest sense, a gateway acts as a bridge between two separate environments. In this case, the gateway bridges the chasm between the IP network and the PSTN.

In a standard VoIP environment, gateways provide the necessary connectivity between the PBX and the IP network for toll-bypass applications. However, gateways play multiple roles in the IP telephony model. Gateways can provide either line-side connectivity (for connecting analog devices such as phones, fax machines, and modems) or trunk-side connectivity for trunks to the public network. Gateways can be analog or digital. They can take the form of a single card (or blade or module) that is housed in an available slot within an Ethernet switch or router. This is an important concept, because a router with an integrated voice trunk card is often mistakenly referred to as a voice-enabled router. This name is inaccurate, because a voice-enabled router actually provides telephony features to end users with IP phones. A gateway, on the other hand, even if it is installed in a router, merely provides an interface from the IP environment to the TDM environment, and vice versa.

A gateway can also be deployed as a standalone component—a chassis that houses multiple trunk cards. Figure 2-4 shows these functional connectivity options for IP telephony gateways. In this example, an analog gateway connects analog phones into the IP network through the network switch.

Figure 2-5 shows how the gateway functionality is incorporated into the network switch and router. In this case, an analog gateway, which connects analog phones to the network, is integrated within the network switch, whereas the digital gateway, which provides PSTN connectivity to the public network, is housed within the router. The approach illustrated in Figure 2-5 is generally a more cost-effective approach for gateway deployments because it is integrated within existing network components.

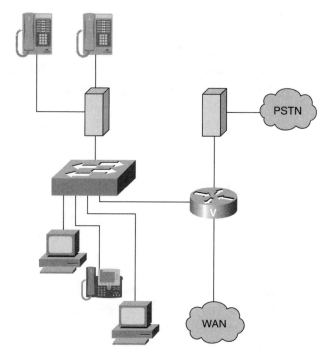

**Figure 2-4** *Connectivity Options for IP Telephony Gateways*

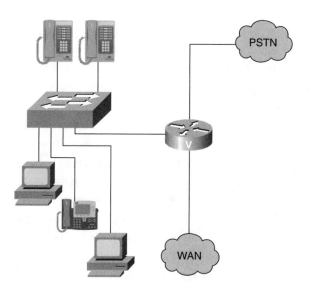

**Figure 2-5** *Analog and Digital Gateways Integrated Within the IP Infrastructure*

Everything in the PBX model is replicated onto the IP network. Line cards on the PBX become switched Ethernet ports on the IP network, which also form the core for the switching environment. Trunk cards from the PBX become gateway ports on the IP network. Gateway ports can be housed within traditional IP components (network routers or Ethernet switches), or in an individual chassis of their own.

# An Efficient Infrastructure

The IPT method of deploying devices and gateway ports is a critical distinction from the PBX, because now the same person (or persons) that support the data hardware environment can now support the voice environment as well.

This is not to advocate the elimination of voice personnel—they are critical enablers for the success of the overall deployment. What this means, however, is that you now have the opportunity to streamline training/learning programs, and to bring new resources to a productive state rapidly because everyone is working on the same infrastructure.

Consider Southwest Airlines as an example. Southwest Airlines has a straightforward business model: short-haul transport of passengers and/or cargo. Its wants to board passengers, get the plane in the air and safely to the destination, drop the passengers off, turn the plane around quickly (maintenance, refueling, restocking, etc.), and board new passengers on the plane quickly so the plane can take off again. This requires a streamlined process that is constant, regardless of which plane is pulling up to the gate, who is flying the plane, who is attending to the plane, or how many passengers are boarding the plane.

To this end, Southwest has a fleet of Boeing 737 aircraft. Itcould have taken the model chosen by other airlines and used a combination of 737s and other aircraft as well, based on the number of passengers expected. However, Southwest's goal is to turn a plane around at the gate in the least amount of time. It wants its planes to spend the majority of the revenue-producing time in the air, not on the ground. To do this, it decided to standardize on one type of aircraft.

This means that all Southwest pilots learn to fly one type of plane. This level of standardization allows the preflight check routine to be consistent for every flight, because there is only one type of aircraft. It means that the flight attendants are always completely familiar with the aircraft. Cleaning the plane between flights is handled quickly and efficiently because the cleaning crew knows each plane thoroughly. The ground crew members only have to worry about maintenance for one type of aircraft, so when potential problems occur, everyone in maintenance knows the plane—they do not have to bring in a 757 specialist or a DC-10 specialist. These standardized processes are consistent in all areas, enabling a rapid turnaround, which is Southwest Airlines' fundamental goal.

Similarly, IP telephony allows customers to standardize their voice and data learning/training plans for personnel. The network equipment, or infrastructure, now can handle both voice and data connectivity. This allows the customer's personnel (or the personnel from their solutions provider) to use the same people to install and manage both the voice and the data aspects of a converged solution, which drives costs down for both parties. New people coming into the company need to learn only one environment, and that environment can support all information requirements—voice, data, and video. This becomes a compelling driver for companies—increased productivity from their support personnel who can now support the overall enterprise as opposed to just one piece of the puzzle.

Finally, the call set-up and release, and the features required for telephony users is replicated on the IP network through the use of a call application on the network. This application is usually housed on a server, and also provides the call detail recording seen within the traditional PBX model. In a Cisco IPT environment, this application and server is referred to as the *CallManager*.

# Bringing New Capabilities to Your Network

The original premise of this chapter still holds true. The PBX in your organization is not broken and works fine just as it is. It has been explained how the functionality of the PBX can be replicated on the IP network, as is, but that does not add anything new to the equation. So the question still needs to be asked and answered: Why replace the PBX with IP telephony? The answer is that IPT brings new capabilities to voice.

Nothing is wrong with your PBX, but your PBX was designed to handle one set of challenges. Today, some 20 years after the launch of the digital PBX, the business landscape has changed. You don't necessarily face the same challenges you did 20 years ago. Competition is different, partners are different, customer expectations are different, and corporate expectations are different. Expectations regarding productivity and return on investment are also different.

As customer requirements change, expand, and become more complex, blending (or converging) voice and data technologies becomes an attractive response to issues organizations face. This convergence is easier and more cost-effective with an IPT approach as opposed to IP-enabling a PBX. The difference lies in the ability of IP telephony to create and support new, converged applications, as opposed to simply allowing voice to traverse the network.

It all begins with the network. The network, with its rich application development and deployment environment, is where organizations attack their business process challenges today. Internet technologies, whether via internal web pages or external websites, provide a flexible and cost-effective means of addressing business issues. Furthermore, the standards-based nature of IP enables organizations to quickly develop and deploy these business-impacting solutions.

IP telephony is designed to take advantage of IP, and networks (internal and external) that use IP as a foundation. This means that applications in an IPT environment are developed quickly and supported with the same resources that organizations and software developers use for their other IP applications. The applications and developers can rapidly adapt to the ever-changing business climate. The IP phone becomes far more than a telephone. It becomes a voice-enabled client that, if desired, can access and interoperate with existing applications as well as new applications yet to be developed. Similarly, a PC or laptop in an IP telephony environment becomes more than just a data workstation. It can become a voice-enabled client that handles the voice, data, and video requirements of the end user. In the end, this means greater flexibility and potentially greater cost savings, with one client at the desktop as opposed to two for selected users.

The explosion of the Internet and Internet technologies have had virtually no impact on the PBX end user. Certainly, browser-based applications are used by the telecommunications support group to manage the PBX. Yet, because of the proprietary, closed nature of the PBX, the ever-increasing impact of the Internet for telephone users has remained nonexistent.

For this reason, most customers, when faced with the potential impact of IP phones running applications, find it difficult to even imagine a use for such a device. Decades of closed architectures and proprietary, closed solutions from PBX manufacturers have served to limit the imaginations of the corporate enterprise when it comes to telephony. To demonstrate this point, here are two examples of how IPT can meet common business needs: virus alerts and paging.

## Virus Alerts

Organizations today face the challenge that viruses pose to the integrity and availability of their networks, and by extension, the information contained within their networks. When a virus hits an e-mail server, consider how the users are typically notified.

Monica sits down at her desk, opens Outlook, starts browsing through messages, and comes across a message from Jerry, her coworker. The header to the message simply says, "Take a look at this."

Monica opens up the e-mail without realizing it contains a virus that Jerry had previously unknowingly spread to other users on his contact list. Now Monica's machine is infected and, unbeknownst to her, the process starts all over again. Monica is unaware that her computer might be infected until she continues to browse her inbox and notices numerous messages from different people, all with the same subject header: "Take a look at this."

Looking further, she sees a message from Scott in the IS department and the header to his message is as follows: "Do Not Open Messages with the Header 'Take a look at this.'"

Sound familiar? You open your e-mail and 20 messages are waiting for you from different people, all with the same header, and you don't notice it until you've opened the first one, and infected your computer.

Now imagine an IP phone: A different type of phone with a large screen and an integrated browser that is able to access and receive information. Imagine walking into your office first thing in the morning, hearing a chirping from your phone speaker, and seeing a message on your phone display, as shown in Figure 2-6.

***Figure 2-6*** *Virus Alerts Generated on an IP Phone*

In this example, the IP phone is a natural conveyer of an alert, or a warning. Users can be notified of potential viruses or problems before they log onto the network, and thereby reduce chances of further proliferation of network viruses. This example demonstrates how IP telephony helps organizations address a different type of challenge—situational alerts, visually and audibly—a challenge that didn't even exist when PBXs were first created.

Perhaps this user not only has an IP phone at work, but also at home. Employees with high-speed Internet service at home can now, through Virtual Private Network (VPN) technology, still access their corporate IP network for both voice and data services. Users with IP phones at home can receive the same alerts as though they were sitting at their desk in the office.

Perhaps this user does not even have an IP phone, but rather, has chosen to deploy an IP software phone client (often called a softphone, or virtual-phone) on his laptop computer. By using a headset, he has turned his mobile laptop into a mobile phone as well, connected to the IP network either directly (in the office) or via high-speed VPN (from the home). Regardless, a virus alert can be sent to the "phone client" on their laptop.

Whether the user has an IP phone or a softphone, and whether he is connected at the office, at home, or in a hotel room, he has the ability to receive alerts and alarms through a new client outside the boundaries and limitations of their e-mail system. IP telephony is not the answer to a company's security requirements—but IPT can, in fact, become an effective tool to help communicate status and alert employees of various real-time scenarios.

Virus protection and user-alerting is a scenario where traditional PBX phones are not designed to handle incoming network-based messages. Certainly, computer telephony integration (CTI) development could create an application where some type of alert could be delivered, probably audibly, to a PBX phone. However, this approach is expensive and difficult to maintain. IP phones, on the other hand, operate on the network and act as any other IP client and, therefore, can be communicated with just like any other IP client using easily deployed, easily updated network-based applications.

In other words, IP phones, as voice-enabled IP clients on the network, are a cost-effective and logical place to alert enterprise users of situations on the network or in the workplace.

## Paging

Let's take the example of paging into the IP telephony environment. Paging is a traditional PBX feature that was created to contact people in a target environment and provide specific information to them. A typical page could be any of the following:

- **All employees in the packaging department please report to the west door.** This is a page that could go across an intercom system to a single speaker, or to a set of PBX phones.

- **Rick, please come to register 7.** This is a page that can likely go across speakers in an entire store, unless the person looking for Rick knows exactly where Rick is at the moment.

- **This is a reminder that the county inspector will be here in 20 minutes.**

Notice that in each of these examples, the page delivered is verbal, or audible in nature, and one-way. In other words, PBX paging is a verbal process that allows one person to page others. However, in an environment where two-way communication is vital, this form of paging falls short of customer requirements.

Today's IPT applications page audibly and visually. These pages come across a phone speaker, but if someone didn't hear or understand the page (which happens often), that person need only look down at his/her phone, and the contents of the page are spelled out visually.

Furthermore, the intended party might not have heard the page. An IP telephony application can enable users to confirm that they heard the page by pressing a button on their phone to indicate acceptance of and compliance to the paged request.

Taken a step further, IP telephony applications allow users to pick up an IP phone, speak the information that needs to be paged, then enter the date and time when the page is to be processed. Reminders can be set (much like on a personal computer or within an e-mail application) and prescheduled to go off (for example, page these 20 phones in the marketing department at 3:30 P.M. tomorrow afternoon).

Finally, IP telephony can also extend paging notification to external people outside the company—if they have a telephone.

# Realizing the Potential of IPT

When talking with clients who initially are skeptical about the role and potential impact of applications running on a telephone, I often use the example of the cellular phone to help remove the blinders that currently block their vision of IP telephony.

Imagine a person with a cell phone that is MSN-enabled. Using his cell phone, the individual can browse the web, download the contact list from his corporate e-mail platform, share images (and potentially video) with other users, and if he gets bored, play some type of game. Yet, the same customers who readily understand this scenario when it relates to a cell phone cannot imagine similar, or even enhanced applications running on their corporate phone because, historically, it was unachievable.

Some people might say, "I already have a personal computer on my desk. Why do I need applications running on my phone?" Because of new productivity requirements, companies are slowly but surely re-examining their desktop phones and demanding new uses for these expensive devices. As with the cell phone, *the end user will decide when* to use the button on an IP phone to launch a certain application, and when to click their mouse to launch a different application on their PC. New types of applications linking voice, video, and data will emerge because of customer demand.

Amazingly, teenagers are walking around with a device that is more powerful (a color, web-browsing, image- and video-enabled, game-playing, chat-enabled cell phone) than the unimaginative device that sits on most corporate desktops. The desktop phone (if it is a traditional digital PBX phone) is not only less powerful than the cell phone, but it costs twice as much!

The challenge facing manufacturers, and the partners they use to bring IP telephony solutions to the market, is to remove the blinders from many decision makers, and awaken the hidden power of IP telephony that currently lies dormant within their organizations.

Several challenges face enterprise organizations today. They must integrate the functionality and flexibility of the IP into everyday telephone usage in their enterprise; consider how new applications running on their network can blend voice and data functionality; and, finally, use these applications to impact their businesses in ways not previously considered. In other words, organizations must bring new capabilities to the enterprise without sacrificing current functionality and current features. This leads to the next question often asked about IP telephony:

What about all of my PBX features?

# CHAPTER 3

# BUT WHAT ABOUT ALL OF MY PBX FEATURES?

The corporate telephone system truly is one of the technological marvels of the modern age. Feature-rich and reliable, it is the one constant in any organization about which virtually no one gives a second thought. Users don't come to work wondering if the telephone system is working. When a person picks up the phone to make a call, they expect to hear a dial tone. This incredibly high standard for availability does not happen by accident.

Inside the telecom organization, where you will find technology professionals dedicated to the upkeep of the PBX, documented processes are in place regarding how to handle almost any circumstance. For example, these professionals have a process for when a user moves or wants new features, as well as for when a new user is brought into the organization or must report a problem. Reports document when all calls were placed or received, including duration.

More than anything else, when companies look at IP telephony, they begin with a feature comparison. They are concerned about losing features during a migration to IPT, and if so, which ones. They are concerned about training their users to take advantage of the features of the new system. They also wonder how managing the new system will differ from managing the existing system.

The average PBX has hundreds of features, such as call transfer. This simple-sounding capability can actually become complex. On the surface, one might describe the call transfer feature as the ability to take a phone call that has just been received and send it (transfer it) to another person. However, it doesn't stop there. When the call is sent to the next person, do you just hang up, or do you stay with the call to announce it to the next user? What about the person who is going to receive the call? What do they hear when the call comes in? What does that person see on the phone (if they have a display phone) that indicates that this is a call being transferred? Do they see who is performing the transfer?

Even features that seem basic and ordinary can carry with them a complex set of conditions that must be considered when migrating to a new telephone system.

This chapter discusses some traditional PBX features and how IPT can enhance them, as well as how an incremental deployment can help improve the training process.

# Assessing the Requirements

Two common concerns surround PBX functionality, and both concerns tend to confuse things somewhat when customers investigate IP telephony as a viable solution within their organization:

- The PBX has hundreds of features and every one of them is critical to the customer's requirements.

- Retraining users on a completely different feature set is not a viable option for most organizations.

The reality is that although most organizations have access to hundreds of features available within their PBX, they generally use only 15–20 features. The challenge is that, from company to company, these 15–20 features are not always the same. The common joke among telecom pundits is that every organization actually only needs five to six features, just not the same five to six from company to company, or even from person to person within a company. Although this might be a bit of an overstatement, it is conceptually correct. The way various employees use their features differs from department to department, even within the same organization.

Retraining is something that companies attempt to do any time they change from one PBX manufacturer to another. For example, if a client with a Nortel PBX for the last 10 years switches to Avaya's PBX, retraining is needed because Avaya's feature set is different, and it is implemented differently. Whenever a new platform is brought in by a different manufacturer, retraining of all telephony users is required. So this is a consistent challenge facing organizations regardless of whether they are considering a PBX or an IP telephony solution.

Consider the following scenario. Jim sits at his desk preparing a document for a market research project. He performs the following tasks:

- Searches the Internet, selects one of the search results, and opens it

- Copies this information and then pastes it into the Word document he is writing

- Continues reading, and sees a matrix of statistics that he can use

- Opens a spreadsheet application (such as Excel) and enters the statistics captured from the website

- Creates a pie chart from the input

- Imports the pie chart into the Word document

- Prints the document and retrieves it from the network printer down the hall

Up to this point, Jim is the model of productivity. He has a wealth of technology available to him and he is flawless in his ability to make full use of this technology. Now, as funny as this might sound, the unthinkable occurs next.

The phone rings. Jim answers. He converses for a moment, and just when he is ready to hang up, the caller asks if Mike is there.

"Sure, he's sitting in his cube down the hallway," replies Jim.

"Can you transfer me?"

"Uh... sure, but just in case I lose you, call Mike at extension 3437."

Sound familiar? (For some of us, this hits close to home.)

On one hand, Jim can work with spreadsheets, word-processing applications, search the web, retrieve results, import them into a desktop application, and print documents to a printer in the building. Yet he is so unsure of the most basic of all telephony features, transferring a call, that he gives Mike's extension to the caller in case he fails in his attempt to transfer the call.

So, on one hand, it is true that there are hundreds of PBX features. On the other hand, whether or not users in the organization actually know how to use them is something entirely different. One could argue that for all the features of the PBX, the majority of users know how to use relatively few of them.

Creating a user base that is more knowledgeable of the feature set can be a significant benefit of an IPT deployment. Indeed, many of the clients who have adopted IPT see their users taking advantage of more of the features of their IP telephony solutions. This trend is based entirely on the manner in which IPT is deployed, rather than ease of use of IPT features. The benefits of incremental deployments are detailed later in this chapter.

# An Enhanced Feature Set

Clearly, there are scenarios where specific features are not only a critical part of a work process, but also well understood and fully used by an organization and its users. Therefore, not only should an effective IP telephony solution support those features that are critical to specific organizations, but it should enhance those features/capabilities as well. Let's examine a few of the traditional PBX features that are common across most organizations, and discover how IP telephony can enhance those features and the work processes they support.

## Time-of-Day Ringing/Routing

Consider how time-of-day ringing can be used in the education industry. Although schools increasingly want telephones in the classrooms (often for security reasons), in most cases, the schools place parameters around how the phones are used. A common PBX feature incorporated into schools is time-of-day ringing (or call routing). In other words, because the teacher is in class teaching most of the day, it is important that outside callers do not interrupt the teaching process. If the front office needs to contact a teacher, they use the intercom system to communicate with the teacher. Outside (and even internal) calls coming in to the classroom need to be blocked during certain hours of the day. Whether those calls roll (or forward) to voice mail or to the front office becomes a choice the school makes.

This feature is absolutely critical to the work process for teachers. IP telephony allows schools to implement this basic feature, and expand upon it as well. With IPT, a teacher determines how calls are handled based not only on time-of-day, but also on caller ID.

Take Mrs. White, who teaches high-school English. The generic parameters block calls from 8 A.M. until 11 A.M., when she is teaching, then open calls between 11 A.M. and 11:40 A.M., which is her lunch period. Then, calls are blocked from 11:40 until 2 P.M. She has a free period from 2 P.M. until 2:40 P.M., so calls are allowed through. From 2:40 until 3:30 P.M. when school ends, call blocking is in effect. This is a traditional way of handling calls for Mrs. White.

Suppose, however, that Mrs. White has placed a call to Timmy's parents. Timmy has been having problems, and she wants to speak with his mom or dad.

Here, IP telephony can offer some enhancements to the traditional PBX feature. An IPT application can be written that personalizes the treatment of Mrs. White's incoming calls. She could pull up a list of students and then highlight, or click on Timmy's name. (She can do this either from a PC workstation or directly on the application-enabled IP phone.) The application would then search a database and find the various phone numbers for Timmy's parents that were captured during student registration. His parents' home number, work numbers, and cell-phone numbers have been stored in the database. After Timmy's profile is marked, Mrs. White can direct the phone system on how she wants a call coming from any of Timmy's parents' numbers handled, even allowing the call to ring through to her classroom during the hours that regular calls are blocked.

## Linking Individual Profiles to Telephony Usage

It is clear that linking individual profiles is a useful feature. Continuing with the education example, because Mrs. White highlighted Timmy's name earlier in the morning, the application looks at the incoming caller ID for all calls and compares the incoming caller numbers to the phone numbers stored under Timmy's profile. If the incoming caller ID is blocked or does not match any of the phone numbers, the traditional time-of-day routing schematic remains in effect and the call forwards to voice mail or the front office during hours that Mrs. White is scheduled to teach. If, however, a match is found between the caller ID and a number in the database for Timmy, something different happens.

Exactly what happens depends on the selections Mrs. White made in the application when she highlighted Timmy's name. Perhaps she wants the call put through, regardless of whether she's in the middle of class. Maybe she wants that call to roll to a voice mailbox where she has left a prerecorded message specifically for Timmy's parents. She can even elect to have the call forwarded to another teacher who has a free period, or to the office with a message on the phone screen indicating the importance of this particular call.

All these possibilities expand on the basic time-of-day routing feature for education. This example demonstrates how IP telephony not only supports traditional features, but allows individual users to customize them, as shown in Figure 3-1.

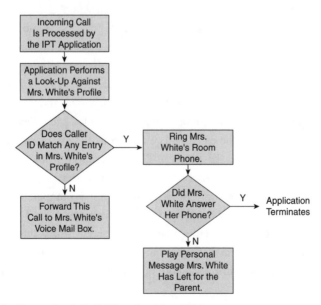

***Figure 3-1*** *Customized Call Flow for Mrs. White*

## Forced Authorization Codes

Another example of a common PBX feature is *forced authorization codes (FAC)*. This feature, when enabled, forces telephony users to enter a predefined code when placing certain types of phone calls, or even all phone calls. This feature has many uses.

A company might have FAC enabled to prevent unauthorized long-distance calls from being placed. In other words, employees of the company who are allowed to make long-distance calls, press 9 (to get an outside line), enter their authorization number, and then dial the number. (Conversely, they could also dial 9, enter the number, and then the authorization code.). The PBX does not connect the call if an invalid code has been entered. In this way, companies control fraudulent use of their long-distance facilities.

A second use for authorization codes is in the legal industry. Law firms make money by billing clients for their time. In a typical law firm, one of the most important applications is the billing system, which allows attorneys to attach their time to specific clients, and bill their clients for phone calls accordingly. Forced authorization codes, in this case, are used for billing purposes. After the attorney enters a code, the call is placed and the PBX attaches the call detail record, which contains information on who placed the call, who they called, and the duration of the call to the authorization code that was entered. So, Jeffrey Johnson places a call to his client, enters an authorization code associated with the client, resulting in the client being billed for the duration of the call.

Forced authorization codes are an example of a feature that one company might use for controlling long distance, whereas another might use it as an integral component of its revenue generation process.

So how can IP telephony enhance this capability? The answer lies in the customization available with IP telephony. In the previous examples, it appears that FAC is an accurate means of tracking calls made by users and preventing fraudulent use of long-distance facilities. In reality, however, specific issues can be raised by this implementation. Suppose, for example, a user enters authorization code 745554231. This is a valid authorization code contained within the PBX database. However, at this point, all we know is that someone has entered a valid code, but we don't know who. For tracking purposes, this can be important.

An alternative is to attach, or link, specific codes with specific extensions, or link specific codes with specific users or departments. It can then be determined who is placing the call, and prevent unauthorized use. This can be accomplished with either a traditional PBX or an IP telephony solution.

In the legal industry, however, the issue becomes more pronounced. For example, the attorney uses the FAC to bill the client. Suppose code 12345 represents ABC Company, and code 12346 represents XYZ Company. Notice that only one digit is different for these two companies. The attorney intending to bill ABC Company might accidentally enter 12346 and end up billing XYZ Company. This inaccuracy clearly presents a billing problem, as well as a customer satisfaction issue.

An IP telephony application solves this problem in a number of ways. Figure 3-2 shows the call flow for a simple validation based on the code entered. The validation occurs *on screen* for the attorney to *see*. In this way, after the attorney enters the authorization code, the application performs a look-up, displays the name of the company to be billed, and then asks for confirmation. The validation process allows for simple, effective, and accurate billing, designed to increase the revenue stream for the law firm.

The look-up can be performed against the corporate database of clients, and therefore not require a specialized database written or created specifically for this use. Or, the look-up could be performed against an individual contact list kept by each of the attorneys. This list could be accessed either from their IP phone display or their PC at their desk. For the attorney working from home with a high-speed Internet connection on her PC and an IP softphone client that allows her to pull up her contact list on the PC, she can still bill her calls to the corporate billing system automatically, with visual confirmation for accuracy.

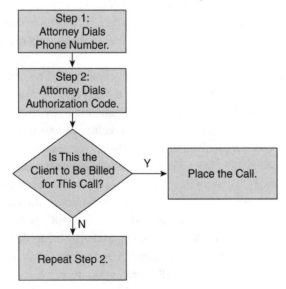

*Figure 3-2*  *Call Flow for Client Billing Validation*

A second (and potentially better) approach is to eliminate the need for entering codes in some cases by performing a look-up on the number dialed instead of the code entered. In other words, the attorney billing ABC Company never enters an authorization code. The attorney simply enters the phone number for ABC Company, and based upon that phone number, the application knows who to bill, as shown in Figure 3-3.

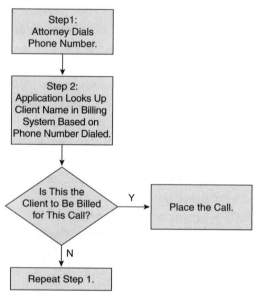

**Figure 3-3**  *Call Validation Based on Number Dialed*

This approach saves keystrokes and is accurate, yet it might present another problem. What happens if the phone number being dialed is not the number the attorney desires to bill? For example, the attorney might dial the number of a witness for a case involving ABC Company. In this situation, they don't want to bill the witness, but need to associate this call with ABC Company.

So, perhaps a combination of Figure 3-2 and Figure 3-3 is a better overall solution. This solution would look at the number dialed, perform a look-up, ask the attorney if this is who they want to bill, and if not, then allow the attorney to enter the code for the correct client to be billed. Another variation would be to provide a name-based search feature so the lawyer doesn't have to know the phone number or the account code. The attorney can use the phone's keypad to enter the first few characters of the client's name. The application then searches the client database and retrieves any matching clients. The attorney then simply presses a button on the phone to associate the call with the selected client.

Still another option, however, is eliminating codes altogether, and use database look-ups as the sole means of validation. In this scenario, the attorney either enters a phone number or presses a button that pulls up a list of clients' phone numbers. The attorney scrolls through the list on the IP phone and finds the name of the client he or she wants to call. Upon pressing the call button, the application asks the attorney if this is who is to be billed for this call. If the answer is yes, the call proceeds. If the answer is no, the application presents another list of clients, and asks the attorney if the billable client is listed. If yes, the attorney scrolls to that client and selects the button that starts the billing process and proceeds with the call. If no, only then is the attorney asked for a FAC.

These examples demonstrate how IP telephony adds a tremendous amount of flexibility to the process of billing clients. It can make the process easier, faster, and more accurate. Furthermore, imagine the call not being made from an IP phone, but rather from an application running on the attorney's PC workstation, as discussed earlier. A representation of two such softphone clients is shown in Figures 3-4 and 3-5. The options are almost endless.

*Figure 3-4* *NetCom System's SoftPhone Representation on a PC Workstation*

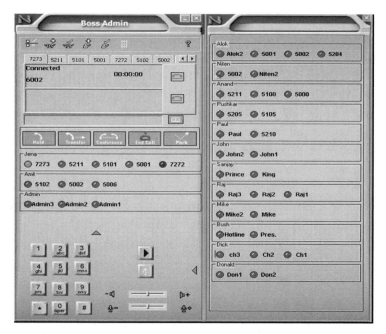

***Figure 3-5*** *Norstan CDG's Boss Admin Secretarial SoftPhone*

The softphone shown in Figure 3-5 is an example of tailoring an IP telephony application to a particular business function—in this case, the secretary's responsibilities to handle the incoming calls for managers. This application supports touch-screen capabilities, which means that the secretary can invoke capabilities by touching the screen as opposed to using a mouse. The right side of this client shows the various managers (and their extensions) that this particular secretary can "see," and enables the secretary, at the touch of a button, to answer/intercept incoming calls for a manager, transfer calls, conference calls, or forward calls to voice mail—all from his/her laptop or desktop PC.

Using the law firm example, consider how functional requirements that are specific to an attorney or paralegal can be developed within a PC-based soft client to enhance how calls are handled, how trunk facilities are accessed, or how billing is optimized. In the example of FAC, this feature can be a precoded button on a software application, linked back to either an authorization database, or even with the back-end billing systems.

The key is that the law firm is not limited by the PBX manufacturer's implementation of FAC. The firm can develop (or have developed) an application specifically tailored to its requirements. This flexibility and speed of development is absolutely consistent with Internet technologies. Only now, with IP telephony, are the benefits of Internet technologies (speed, flexibility, standards-based, and low cost) made available to the traditional voice user.

For now, it is assumed that as the PBX continues to evolve, emphasis will be placed on feature preservation and investment protection. As companies migrate from one PBX to the next, feature preservation is of great importance because it simplifies the task of training users on a new system. Furthermore, as the PBX evolves, new capabilities are introduced, but the focus is placed on a gradual introduction of change into the equation.

# An Improved Training Process

Features are important, but users have to know how to actually use the features the company has deployed. Recall the example where Jim, the model of productivity, is a competent user of technology, yet he cannot confidently transfer a call. This is the traditional trend in the corporate environment; the company installs a new telephone system and schedules training, but few come, and even fewer read their User Guides. The question becomes simply this:

What are companies doing to ensure their employees know how to use the technology in which the company has just made a six- or possibly seven-figure decision? More importantly, how can IP telephony affect this trend?

The answer lies not in effort, but process. The training struggle is a result of a traditional PBX technology in which the process dictates that it be deployed literally in a flash—hence the term *flash cut*, which describes the process of turning off one phone system and turning on the new one over a weekend.

When a new telephone system is installed, a new technology has been placed on the desktop of every employee. The problem isn't that some users have to be trained, it's that all users have to be trained at roughly the same time. It's a challenging task when the telecom organization has to train hundreds (or even thousands) of employees in a short period of time, and even tougher when people don't show up for training. Often, when classes are rescheduled, people still miss the make-up session. At some point, the telecom organization has to move away from the training requirement and focus on maintaining the high availability requirements of voice communications. Therein lies the problem. The company is left with a new technology, limited resources who know how to use the technology, and a telecom organization that is now focused on maintaining the technology.

IP telephony solves the training issue not through technology, but through process. IP phones are not inherently easier to use than traditional phones. In fact, one could argue that because IP phones can do more than a PBX phone, they are, in fact, more difficult to use. Although this thinking is logical, it is not entirely true. Ensuring that employees are fully productive with this new technology is of prime importance. The answer is in how IP telephony can be deployed.

Let's compare a traditional PBX deployment with a potential IPT deployment.

Figure 3-6 depicts a traditional PBX deployment. As discussed previously, this is a flash-cut process; i.e., one system is turned off and the other turned on—usually over a weekend. The company goes from one environment to another, literally overnight, with no interim or intermediate step.

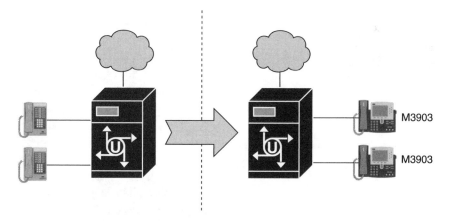

*Figure 3-6* *Traditional Flash Cut from Old PBX to a New PBX*

In this example, training for new users begins when they get their new phone. The problem is that when they get their new phone, the new system is already live and in production. This allows for only a short span of time where the telecom organization can focus on training users before they have to move on to the task of maintaining and managing the system, i.e., keeping it up and running, changing user configurations, handling employee moves, adds and changes, etc.

An easier approach to training would be possible if the company could somehow bring the new technology in-house while the existing technology was still in place. Furthermore, it would be helpful to extend the training timeline to allow months to train employees instead of days. IP telephony, through what is referred to as an incremental deployment, enables this transitory period.

In Figure 3-7, which depicts an IP telephony incremental deployment, there is an interim step during the deployment process. This is referred to as an incremental deployment because the employees of the organization are incrementally migrated (or deployed) from the traditional PBX to the new IPT solution.

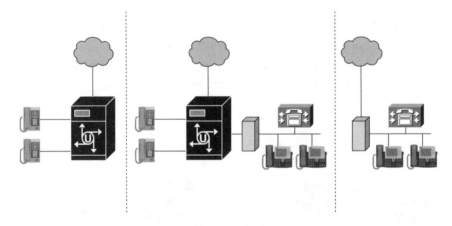

*Figure 3-7* *Incremental Deployment of IP Telephony*

Notice that an incremental deployment is a three-phase approach. Phase 1 shows the traditional PBX environment that is being replaced. In Phase 2, an IP telephony call server is added to the network, along with a gateway. The call server handles the traditional PBX functions for an IPT environment.

In Phase 2, new IP phones become part of the network. These represent a limited number of employees who have been selected to initially migrate to the IP network. Notice how there are now users connected to the PBX, and users connected to the network-based call server.

The gateway shown provides the connection back to the PBX, which allows employees connected to the PBX and employees connected to the network to continue to call each other. Furthermore, they continue to use three-, four-, or five-digit dialing, whichever was used with the PBX system. In this way, only the new users who have a new phone have encountered any change. Otherwise, everyone else continues to communicate with one another as they did previously. Users of the IPT solution on the network use the trunks from the PBX to make and receive external calls. The gateway provides the connection back to the PBX trunk facilities.

The benefit of this incremental approach is that the organization deploying the new telephony technology can decide how many users should migrate to the new environment, and how quickly this migration should occur. For example, Company A might have 500 employees on its PBX in Houston, Texas. It makes the decision to migrate to an IP telephony solution, and identify the first 50 employees who will move from the corporate PBX. The company deploys a relatively inexpensive call server, installs a gateway between the PBX and the call server on the network, and gives these 50 users new phones connected to network switches.

Now these 50 users each have a new phone, and it looks like the training nightmare is ready to begin. The difference is that right now, only 50 users need to be trained, not the entire 500! This is the benefit of an incremental deployment: a few weeks to train these 50 users on the new feature set and the new applications (and identify new applications based on the users' requirements). After a few weeks, the company identifies the next 50 or so employees, perhaps migrating users in a department-by-department approach. These employees receive new phones and training next. A month later, another 50 or so employees migrate, and so on, until all 500 employees have new phones, and at that time, the old PBX is removed from service.

How quickly (or slowly) the company decides to migrate users, and how many are migrated at one time is entirely the company's choice. The technology enables this because it does not require an entire new PBX that supports 500 users immediately. Instead, a server that supports 50 users can be brought in. With IP telephony, the company can continue adding to this solution (without changing out servers) and grow the environment at its own pace.

At the end of the day, most companies deploying IP telephony indicate that their users are better trained and ready to take advantage of the new technology. This is not because the technology is easier to use or easier to learn, but because the *process* by which the new technology is deployed is easier and more cost-effective, and the process for training employees is more flexible and realistic.

So in the end, the question "What about my features?" can actually be better addressed by an IP telephony solution. The IPT solution has proven to produce users who actually know how to transfer, conference, forward, camp on, redial, park, and pick up calls with more confidence and fewer errors than ever before. This, in turn, creates a more productive employee, which is one of the major design goals of an IP telephony solution.

Not only is the IPT technology different from that of a PBX, but how this technology is deployed is different also. Increasingly, IP telephony is looking less like a PBX than originally believed. So, if it is not a PBX, what is it?

# CHAPTER 4

# IF THIS ISN'T A PBX, WHAT IS IT?

The previous chapter concluded by comparing dramatic differences between the PBX and IP telephony. The technologies are different, how they are deployed is different, and *why* they are deployed is different.

The industry has tried to categorize or label IP telephony as merely a new kind of PBX but, in fact, IPT is a stark change from the PBX technology. The evolution of the PBX has confused things somewhat regarding IP telephony. More specifically, the term IP-PBX has done a tremendous disservice to the IP telephony movement. Referring to IP telephony as an IP-PBX places significant limits on the expectations people have of IPT.

A good analogy is the minivan. When the minivan was first introduced, it was somewhat difficult to classify. Was this a new type of car, a new kind of station wagon, or a new type of truck? (Sports utility vehicles, or SUVs, initially saw a similar reaction when they were introduced.) In the end, the minivan became its *own* classification, because it could not be accurately defined by its predecessors. It did not fit into the categories previously available. The same is true with IP telephony.

This chapter focuses on the differences between the traditional TDM PBX and an IP telephony environment. IP telephony is engineered differently, deployed differently, and can provide a new wealth of business-impacting applications. In some cases, the differences between IPT and a PBX are subtle; in other cases, the differences are more dramatic.

The IP telephony market today offers two different approaches for companies to consider. The first approach is the IP-enabled approach championed by PBX manufacturers. This approach has brought the concept of an IP-PBX to the market. The foundation for this offering is the PBX and its feature set. The notion is to take the PBX, and that feature set, and place it on the IP network.

By definition, an IP-PBX is a new type of PBX. It is the latest in a succession of PBXs. It takes the PBX as is, and places it on the IP network—no enhancements, no new capabilities. Same PBX, same PBX features, same PBX *limitations*, but now residing on a new infrastructure. Those who question *why* anyone would want to put their PBX on the network ask a good question. After all, continually lower prices being charged by long-distance carriers have rendered toll-bypass barely significant in many cases.

The second approach, which is the primary focus of this book, is often referred to as the *IP-centric* approach. In this case, the foundation for this offering is not the PBX or its features, but the IP network itself. The IP network becomes the starting point and voice capabilities are built upon this foundation, using the natural, basic building blocks of the network itself.

In the IP-centric approach, IP telephony is not just another PBX. Actually, the term *IP-PBX* is an incorrect assessment of the IP-centric approach. It is not merely the latest enhancement in an evolution of the PBX technology. In fact, it is a pronounced break away from the PBX. Consider the meaning of the name, PBX: Private Branch Exchange.

# The IPT Architecture

Much discussion revolves around whether IP telephony is an evolutionary technology or a revolutionary technology. The truth is that it is a bit of both. Consider the following two statements:

- The idea of an intelligent, open-standards, network-browsing, data-capable *phone* on the desktop is revolutionary.

- The idea of an intelligent, open-standards, network-browsing, data-capable *workstation* on the desktop is not only *not* revolutionary, it is expected and considered commonplace in corporations.

From the perspective of the traditional telephony and voice telecommunications world, IP telephony is clearly revolutionary. We are seeing technology on the desktops that most manufacturers of voice instruments didn't foresee for this timeframe. This is evident in the fact that the initial IP phone offering from virtually every manufacturer still looked and operated like a regular phone, with no advanced capabilities. Network-browsing, Lightweight Directory Access Protocol (LDAP) support, and integrated switching all came with subsequent releases.

However, if you change the perspective from voice to data, and look at it from the view of the IP network, IP telephony is *evolutionary*. Since the advent of the LAN and open standards, there has been a gradual evolution in terms of clients supported on the network. Large desktop personal computers have evolved into large, portable machines, which evolved into compact laptops, which have evolved into hand-held Personal Digital Assistants (PDAs), tablet PCs, and now IP phones. Each is just a client on the network, capable of handling network requirements, but each brings something new to the table for users. Portability, pocket portability, wireless capabilities, video, and now enterprise voice capabilities are all expectations for the myriad of clients available for network deployment.

IP telephony extends the client requirements for IP technologies by providing an open, rules-based environment for how telephony should be handled on the network. Existing standards, such as H.323, and emerging standards, such as Session Initiation Protocol (SIP), continue to lay the groundwork for how telephony can be quickly and cost-effectively deployed as an integrated component within an IP network. These protocols govern how users with diverse requirements—such as mobility, collaboration, or video—can place phone calls as a client or member of the network.

## An Open Environment

None of the three words that define a PBX, or Private Branch Exchange, accurately describe IP telephony. There is nothing private about IP telephony. It is an open environment, based increasingly on industry standards.

There is nothing branch-oriented about IP telephony. The PBX was originally designed to work as a *single*, *isolated* system at a *single* location. Later enhancements enabled PBXs to communicate with other PBXs across an enterprise. In most cases, the PBXs used proprietary protocols (Cornet-D as an example in the Siemens world). In other cases, some protocols have become pseudo-standards. The ITU-T recommendations for ISDN signaling systems (QSIG) is an example of this. QSIG is a peer-to-peer signaling system used in corporate voice networking solutions that provides a standard method for transporting features transparently across a network.

The best-known standard would be ISDN PRI or T1 connections, but even then, some vendors enhance these links, which again makes them proprietary. The PBX industry had to work at enabling seamless integration between disparate systems in order for them to communicate with one another across an enterprise and appear as one system.

Conversely, IP telephony assumes from the beginning that an enterprise-wide solution is the desired result. A true, native IPT solution is designed, from its inception, to be distributed across an enterprise, cost effectively, with no loss of feature or function. Further, with IP telephony, *inter*-site communication between multiple locations is designed to be a natural extension of *intra*-site communications.

## Enterprise-Oriented

An IP telephony solution uses the IP network to extend full voice capabilities throughout the enterprise. Managing calls site-to-site across the enterprise is inherently designed within IP telephony, therefore, no special protocols or enhancements to the basic solution are needed. Seamless deployment of new users and new clients across the enterprise is designed within the framework of IPT. Extending IPT throughout a network, with proper planning, due diligence, and system design, can be as easy as plugging a phone into a wall jack. Literally.

Figure 4-1 shows the Cisco Systems view of IP telephony. This diagram demonstrates how a centralized call server, referred to as CallManager, provides PBX telephony features and functionality for all locations on the network. Notice that in this environment, it is not necessary to replicate these servers, or boxes, at each location. After the telephony server application is implemented on the network, the network ensures that all resources attached to the network can access the telephony functions.

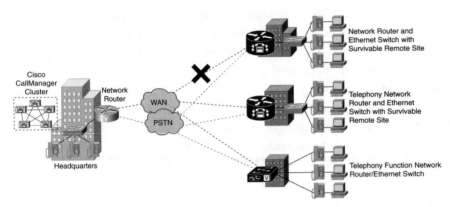

*Figure 4-1*  *Cisco IP Telephony Extended Across an Enterprise*

As shown in Figure 4-1, the notion of an IP-based solution that is private and branch-oriented is a completely inaccurate description of the intrinsic nature of IP telephony.

Because of this, some might ask the question, "Can IP telephony work effectively in a single location?" The answer is yes. The following statement describes it best: IP telephony is inherently designed—and able—to cost-effectively provide converged voice and data features, services, and applications across an enterprise, whether the enterprise is a single location, or hundreds of locations.

Now, although it is true that an IP telephony solution must replicate many of the functions of a PBX to provide voice services, the objective of IPT is not to simply reproduce the PBX on the network. As Richard Platt constantly reminded everyone at Selsius Systems, "With IP telephony, the network *is* the PBX." This mindset produced a different kind of product. It forced IP telephony developers at Selsius Systems to introduce something new into the picture—applications—or more specifically, an environment where applications could be easily called into play.

## Not a Phone, But a Client

Fundamentally, IP telephony does not consider desktop instruments to be phones, but rather clients. More than anything else, it is this difference in perspective that drives IPT away from the traditional PBX technologies. In a PBX, we have fax machines and modems, and we have telephones at the desktop. These phones can be analog, digital, or even wireless for mobile employees. The focus for these PBX instruments is a feature set driven by the administrator of the overall system.

On an IP network, however, we have clients at the desktop. These clients can be desktop computers, laptop computers, wireless PDAs, wireless laptops, printers, fax machines, and now with IP telephony, IP phones. Each of these clients is designed, by obeying the rules of the IP network, to interact with one another. So we begin to think of an IP phone more as an IP client designed to access network applications *and* place and receive phone calls.

# Customized, Focused Applications

Making phone calls is an obvious requirement for IP telephony, but taken to its natural conclusion, it brings new capabilities and new features to an organization. These new capabilities, as noted in the education example in Chapter 3, "But What About All My PBX Features?," tend to be focused on and customized to a particular organization and their requirements.

Although manufacturers of an IP-PBX tend to view the IP network as nothing more than plumbing, manufacturers of true IP telephony see the network as the reason for moving to telephony in the first place. That is where the applications are, and applications will be the defining factor for most organizations looking at IPT in the future.

Consider the three widely accepted benefits of an IP-PBX. It reduces costs associated with system maintenance, system administration, and Moves, Adds and Changes (MAC) for user administration. It reduces long-distance charges and it potentially helps consolidate resources between the IS and telecom departments.

Notice, however, that each of these benefits target resources and budgets within the IS or the telecom department. Rarely do these benefits step outside the budgets of either one of these departments. The following examples show how IPT can benefit areas outside of the IS or telecom departments.

## Secondary Schools

Consider a high school that implements an IP telephony solution. Rather than focus on cost reductions (which incidentally, will be realized anyway), many high schools today are focusing on the specific challenges they face.

Frederick County Public Schools in Virginia, for example, chose to deploy IP telephony as a means of enhancing the process teachers use to take attendance and issue hall passes. This example will be discussed in greater detail in Chapter 5, "Focusing on the Few", but it is important to realize that this school was looking for more than dial tone on the network. Their objective was not limited to taking their existing voice requirements and putting them on the network. They were looking for (and found, in IP telephony) a more accurate and faster means of taking student attendance, and a more secure means of issuing hall passes.

Notice in these examples (attendance tracking and issuance of hall passes), the beneficiary at the school is not the IS department or the telecom department, but rather the teachers and, as detailed later, the overall security of the school.

Figure 4-2 is a screen shot from an IP telephony application written by AAC, a third-party developer for Cisco AVVID applications. This is an example of a confirmation displayed on the IP phone when a teacher has successfully created a hall pass for a student, Bob Chilcote. The hall pass was created on the IP phone by the teacher, and can be accessed in any number of ways by authorized school personnel.

Ironically, advances in technology are one of the reasons many schools see phone-initiated electronic hall passes as not only a convenient application, but also an increasingly necessary one. Because of technology advances and decreasing prices, many students have access to a personal computer in their homes. With this access, schools are finding out, students can be enterprising little creatures, to say the least.

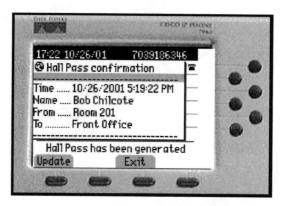

***Figure 4-2*** *IP Telephony Application Issuing School Hall Passes*

Today's students are increasingly proficient in PC applications, to the extent that some now show up to school with their *de facto* hall pass in hand. These students have realized that all that is needed to create a hall pass is a decent understanding of Microsoft Word, or PowerPoint, and a color printer. Armed with these tools (and at least one genuine hall pass from which to copy), creating a hall pass is child's play for a young teen who is computer-savvy enough to surf the web, download music files, share digital pictures and instant messages with friends.

This is the reality that schools face today—a student clientele that understands computers as much, if not better than school officials. Sometimes, this is humorous. Often, however, it can take a decidedly more serious turn. Students loitering in the halls is more of a security risk today than it was 10 or 20 years ago, and IP telephony applications are increasingly becoming tools to deal with this new reality.

## Rail Transportation

Another IP telephony developer, NetCom Systems (which has recently been acquired by Norstan Communications, Inc.), has developed an application that helps customers with offices in urban areas that use rail transportation. Consider the number of people who use public rail transportation as a means of getting to and from the workplace. As shown in Figure 4-3, NetCom's application, called IP-Rail, allows users to get an up-to-date transportation schedule for their desired route at the touch of a button. This application, although simple in concept, actually provides a great service to the East Coast employees for whom it was written. Applications such as this can be written to enable users to get quick access to information, potentially purchase products at the touch of a button, and with another touch of a button, initiate a live conversation with someone for assistance—all from the desktop phone in their office.

*Figure 4-3* *NetCom Systems IP-Rail Application for IP Phones*

At first glance, you might ask, "Why couldn't this information be accessed from the user's desktop personal computer?" The obvious answer is that users certainly could use their PCs for this application. However, most of the time, the user is going to think of checking the schedules after they have already closed their PC down, and have it loaded into their attaché-case and are ready to head out the door. In this scenario, all that is needed is one touch on the phone, and the information is readily available.

## Sales and Professional Services

Sue is an account executive operating out of a cube at the regional building of a sales organization. Her extension is 3201. It is currently 9:45 in the morning. Ray, her husband, places a call to her extension, and this incoming call interacts with her personal calendar on her desktop computer. A network application looks at her calendar to see if she is available and determines that she is off-site with one of her distributors from 9 a.m. until 11 a.m. The application looks at the incoming automatic number identification (ANI, or calling party information) of the caller, and does a quick look-up against Sue's personal list. It matches the number with Ray's cell phone. The rules in her calendar tell the application that any call from Ray between 9 a.m. and 11 a.m. should automatically be forwarded to her pager.

Minutes later, Rick, a sales peer, also calls her. The application checks her calendar again, and seeing she is out and no rules were entered for Rick, the application forwards Rick to her voice mailbox.

Finally, Sue's boss Julia calls at 10:05 a.m. Again, the application checks Sue's whereabouts, matches Julia's number, and based on the rules Sue entered, automatically interrupts Sue by ringing her cell phone.

All this happened because of events that Sue told her personal call-processing application to look for. In this case, the system-wide telephony solution interoperated with Sue's personal call-handling application and her personal calendar. This occurred seamlessly, without any proprietary protocols, black boxes, or unsupported code. As easily as Word and Excel interoperate and exchange information, so can IP telephony applications be written to do essentially the same thing.

Furthermore, the originating source or the destination of such applications does not have to be the IP phones themselves. As demonstrated in the example with Sue, the application governing how calls are presented to her can be an application running in the background on the network. She can enter thresholds or parameters directly into her corporate e-mail/calendar page, or into a new desktop application that interfaces with her e-mail, or directly into a new screen on her IP phone.

You can see how applications introduced by IP telephony can be networked-based, desktop-based, or IP phone-based. Put a different way, these new applications place the control over how everyday calls are processed into the hands of the employee at the desktop, and give the employee access to virtually any information on the network (or off the network) at the touch of a button on their phone.

To describe this kind of one-touch access, Bob Richter at Hartford Independent School district coined the term *speed URLs*. Traditional telephones have speed dials, which are special buttons that perform specific tasks (such as one-touch calling to specific phone numbers). IP telephony, through the use of speed URLs, extends this capability beyond one-touch dialing to actually provide one-touch access to specific applications (and/or information contained within a server or database). How this information is used, and how it can be incorporated into daily call routines, is customizable from company to company.

As you can see, IP telephony actually provides an opportunity to bring new features and applications to an organization. Although it embraces the telephony functions—such as hold, connect, transfer, camp-on, do-not-disturb, park, and pick-up—it also enables new, interactive features, such as access to specific information sources that might reside on your corporate network, or even in the public Internet. In addition, it enables the development of applications that can handle customized call handling on a user-by-user basis.

Clearly, for employees who do not have a PC or other data workstation, this is an ideal environment—their phone becomes an intelligent network client capable of accessing, processing, and displaying information. However, even for those employees who do have a PC at their desk, IP applications on the phone can be useful. These benefits are detailed in Chapter 5.

# The Power of Convergence

On the surface, Figure 4-4 seems oddly misplaced in a discussion about IP telephony and convergence. In fact, it is a picture that I often have used in initial discussions with senior leaders in an organization when talking about convergence.

*Figure 4-4*  *Pre-Convergence (Circa 1970s)*

In looking at this picture, I like people to ask themselves one question: How have data and voice technologies changed since this picture was taken, and how has the way we use them changed? As they start to answer this question for themselves, the entire point of IP telephony and convergence comes clearly into focus. Imagine the office environment of the 1970s. The office had a large computer monitor, a huge keyboard, and of course, a telephone. So, the question stands: What has changed in the last 30 or so years?

Certainly the monitor has changed. In the 1970s, monitors were monochrome: The two choices were amber on black or green on black. Color? Not even an option yet. Think about what was not here. This desktop computer was tied to a mainframe computer somewhere. Most people recognize how the advances in chip and silicon technology have not only helped reduce costs, but also dramatically decreased the size of computers. Rewind 30 years and imagine the sheer size of the mainframe computer running things in this picture.

The Windows environment did not exist. In fact, there was no DOS environment either, because the PC had not even been introduced. So, no mouse, no sound card, no departmental printers, no Virtual Private Network (VPN), no digital subscriber line (DSL), no cable modem; in fact, no way for the employee to work at home effectively. There was no Internet access, internal or external. Also, no word processing, no spreadsheets, no personal databases, no color, no color graphics.

Since the 1970s, the following products have been introduced to the market:

- Personal computers (desktop and laptop) with new models introduced every year
- PDAs
- Color monitors with incredible graphics and sound
- Departmental minicomputers, which gave way to LANs with the advent of Ethernet
- Local printing
- Internet access, both internal and external
- Microsoft Windows
- The mouse
- Word processing, spreadsheets, slide presentations with LCD panels
- Desktop video (streaming and downloadable)
- Remote high-speed access via cable modems and DSL
- VPN tunneling into corporate networks
- Off-the-shelf applications replacing IS-developed programs

This is just the short list. So much has changed in the data realm of technology as it relates to corporate usage. How data is used and the tools available to users has changed dramatically, not just in the past 30 years, but in the past 5 years. That is the ongoing reality of data technologies.

Now, consider the other instrument on the desktop in the picture—the telephone—and ask the same question. What has changed in the past 30 or so years, in how this technology is used in the corporate environment?

Many businesses now have advanced call centers, but this doesn't affect most end users. Voice mail has certainly made a tremendous impact, as have interactive voice recognition (IVR) technologies. The most prolific advancement, the cell phone, may or may not be a corporate-initiated tool.

For the most part, the company-provided, desktop telephone in the workplace is used the same way it was 20 or 30 years ago. Although a standard PBX offers hundreds of features, the average user still uses only a handful of them. PBXs are deployed the same way today as they were in the 1970s—in a flash-cut mode, where the entire system is cut over (installed and brought into production) over a weekend, or overnight.

Also, PBX technology remains proprietary. Whereas you might see numerous kinds of PCs and workstations on a Cisco data network—in the form of Dell, IBM, Compaq, Apple, Gateway, HP, etc.—you still today won't see a Nortel digital phone running on a Siemens PBX, or an Avaya digital phone on a Nortel PBX. New, faster, more powerful PCs and other data clients, such as PDAs, come to the market annually. New Ethernet switches, routers, and access units (combo switch/ routers) are launched every year. However, new digital phones from their various manufacturers come to the market much more infrequently.

These points are important because convergence changes this model. Already, an explosion of IP phones are hitting the market almost at the same rate that PCs are coming to market, and certainly much faster than traditional phones. Soon, IP phone advancements will match what is happening in the cellular phone market.

This means the time-to-market for convergence clients such as IP phones is going to be much faster, and this of course, is good for the market. We, as companies and end users of companies, are going to have a wider choice of devices, and those choices are going to change/increase more rapidly than we are accustomed to for phones. Technology advances in phones will proceed at the same rate as technology advancements in other data clients.

As of this writing, for example, I hold in my possession a small-sized cell phone that is voice-activated. It is capable of exchanging text messages and equipped with voice messaging. When I purchased this cell phone, it was considered fairly top-of-the-line. Today, less than a year later, it is absolutely obsolete—it does not surf the web, download personal profiles, and (gasp) does not have a color screen! In some circles, this small, compact, and usable technology is considered something of a relic. This is what is in store for IP phones in the coming years. This is a somewhat uncomfortable situation for people who are accustomed to the business voice environment being much more static, but this type of change is what convergence delivers to the market. The Cisco IP telephony offerings are a perfect example of this trend.

The Cisco IP phones in 1998 were basically Intecom digital phone plastics with an Ethernet hub inside. At first glance, one could not look at a Selsius Systems IP phone and see any difference between it and a digital business phone available from any other manufacturer. A year later, a new IP phone with a switch inside and a much larger display was launched. Immediately, this new phone was seen as different. People wondered why the need for such a large screen for a telephone. The answer came within months of this phone's introduction. Phone-based Extensible Markup Language (XML) support for application development was added, as was support for LDAP. Within a year, two more phone models were added, and a year later brought yet another model.

At the time of this writing, Cisco is already briefing customers about the next generation of IP phones, due in the 2003–2004 time frame, which includes a larger color screen, touch-screen capabilities, and video support. This is just an example of Cisco Systems products. New IP phones on the market from various manufacturers already include stylus pencils, integrated card readers, and security devices for military applications. Figure 4-5 shows the evolution of Cisco phones since 1998, which clearly articulates this point.

| 1998 | 1999 | 2000 | 2002 |
| --- | --- | --- | --- |
| 12SP+ | 30VIP | 7940/7960 | 7905 |

**Figure 4-5**  *Evolution of Cisco IP Phones*

There are two primary benefits to companies who adopt a convergence strategy. The first is new desktop voice technology advancing at the same rate as has been seen with data devices, running applications as easily as data devices, and therefore impacting business processes as effectively as data devices. The previous description of electronic hall passes for schools is an example of how advancing technology can have an impact on issues that an organization (in this case, schools) might face.

The second benefit is far more subtle, yet just as important. Chapter 7 deals with the subject of preparing for IP telephony deployments, and explains what usually needs to be done to get an organization, and more specifically, an organization's network, ready to run voice sessions and IPT applications.

## A More Robust Network

Most preexisting networks today are not ready to run voice applications without modifications. Often, these modifications can be significant. New standards of network availability and performance must be achieved in order to deliver the same level of reliability to which voice users are accustomed. New processes for implementing new capabilities on the network without impacting user availability are required, because users do not accept any downtime for the phones. At the end of the day, most customers who successfully deploy IP telephony agree that their IP networks are much more sound, more robust, and far more available than ever before, and that can be attributed to what was necessary to get their networks ready to run voice applications.

| NOTE | The two major benefits of a convergence initiative are the rapid introduction of business-impacting voice technologies into an organization, and the ultimate result of a fortified, highly resilient, and secure network with new processes for managing high-availability for all network-based solutions. |
| --- | --- |

New applications are going to be an absolute requirement for IP telephony to truly become a mainstream, business-impacting technology. As stated at the end of Chapter 1, "Haven't We Been Here Before?," convergence is all about change. Let's revisit this concept, because this is the litmus test for companies looking at convergence and IP telephony.

## Incremental Deployments

As previously mentioned, convergence is going to challenge the traditional thinking that goes on inside corporations. How companies deploy technologies, the expectations they have for voice technologies, and how they ultimately support these new technologies is undergoing dramatic change. This makes many people uncomfortable because of the misconceptions surrounding IP telephony.

Part of the change begins with how this technology can be deployed. Clearly, one of the major initial benefits of IPT is that it can be deployed incrementally. Corporations have the opportunity to protect (and if desired, expand) the investment already made in TDM technology *while at the same time* beginning to deploy IP telephony in a cost-effective manner. This approach is similar to what happened in the 1980's migration from centralized mainframes to LAN-based solutions, as shown in Figure 4-6.

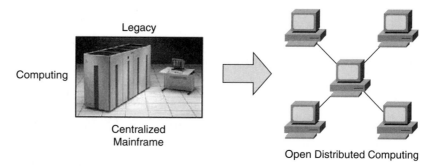

Legacy

Computing

Centralized
Mainframe

Open Distributed Computing

*Figure 4-6* *Migration from Mainframes to Distributed LANs*

Think back to when organizations first began migrating from mainframe computers to LANs: No one threw their mainframe out the front door right away. Indeed, many companies today still have both mainframe computers and LANs in place. Organizations, department by department, migrated (or transitioned) their users from being mainframe-connected to becoming LAN-connected. After users were connected to the LAN with a new "workstation" (the personal computer), they still had to maintain connectivity for that workstation back to the original mainframe. This enabled users to access their existing applications, while taking advantage of new ones that were more departmental, or even local to their machine.

As new applications became available, end users began to depend more on their local PC and departmental servers, and less on the traditional applications on the mainframe.

Subsequently, many of the mainframe-based applications were migrated to the LAN environment with enhancements. In the end, some companies eventually did away with their mainframes, and others still use both mainframes and LAN applications to serve their employees and customers.

The methodology for migrating from one data environment to another was demonstrated in clear terms in the 1980s and 1990s. Now, much of the same thing is happening. The mainframe has been replaced by the PBX. The distributed LAN is replaced by distributed IP telephony. Yet, the methodology that was proven in the earlier migration remains the same:

- In the 1980s, the older 3270 terminals were replaced by personal computers. Today, older PBX phones are being replaced by IP phone clients.

- In the 1980s, personal computers were taken off the mainframe (with their 3270 emulator cards) and placed on the LAN. Today, new IP phones are being placed directly on the LAN (IP network).

- Finally, in the 1980s, LAN workstations were provided access back to the mainframe environment and its applications by means of a gateway. Today, a new kind of gateway provides connectivity for LAN-based telephony users to access resources back on the PBX.

The technical merits, challenges, and solutions of migration strategies are explored in Chapter 7, "Watch That First Step"; however, it bears noting that this technology was designed, from its inception, to be migrated into a customer environment following the methodology learned from the mainframe-LAN transition.

Just as the expectation was not to completely remove one's mainframe computer immediately, the expectation for IP telephony is that companies will not want to replace their PBXs completely all at once—because they don't have to.

This sounds fairly simplistic, but the truth of the matter is that this has never happened before with voice communications. The procedure has always been to buy a PBX and flash cut it over a weekend, or overnight. The financial investment was a replacement investment; that is, companies had to invest enough to replace the entire system.

Now, however, IP phones can be deployed into an organization individually, or departmentally, as is the case with other IP clients, such as PCs or printers. IP phones can be implemented on the IP network and allowed to coexist with the traditional PBX phones, just as was done with PCs and mainframes. This means that a company can begin deploying a new phone system—a new telecommunications solution—into their organization a piece at a time. This is something that has not been cost-effectively done with traditional PBXs. Instead of a replacement investment, IP telephony enables companies to make transition investments; for example, investing only in the technology required to migrate $x$ number of users, where $x$ is considerably less than the entire organization, and is determined by the customer.

This manageable and measurable approach can turn the stressful event of cutting hundreds or thousands of phones and users into an easily managed process that can take as little or as much time as the organization decides. This approach has become a time-tested methodology within the IP telephony market in the past few years.

Consider the fact that Cisco Systems took almost 3 years to migrate all 23,000-plus of its employees in its San Jose campus environment away from its legacy PBX to IP telephony. In January 2003, Cisco cut over the final piece of TDM switching from their Lucent Definity system to the Cisco AVVID IP telephony solution. This project began in 1999, and it followed the incremental migration model. Cisco went department by department, building by building, learning from each deployment and adjusting accordingly. For Cisco Systems, the potentially daunting task of moving from TDM to IP became an easily managed process.

This is the new model for deploying telephony. For a period of time, two different environments are supported instead of one. Usually, one of those environments is new for the people providing support. The telecom staff must become familiar with IP, and the IS staff must become familiar with voice.

Subsequently, that familiarity must lead to true competency. An incremental deployment, or migration, allows this learning inside the organization to happen gradually, at a pace comfortable for the personnel involved. Everything becomes incremental: learning, spending, training, and ultimately, deployments.

This methodology also provides a tremendous cultural benefit to the organization. It allows the IS and telecom groups to learn to work together, and clearly shows each group that one is not a threat to the other. Both groups remain essential to the success of the organization.

| NOTE | The concept of an incremental deployment is simple: If you don't have to spend, train, and learn how to support technology investments all at once, then don't. |
|------|---|

At Selsius Systems, the thought process was always to allow customers to migrate at their own pace so they could learn at their own pace. Corporations could invest in an incremental fashion. From the Selsius perspective, this was always the primary initial benefit of IP telephony. As more companies begin the road to convergence, it will be with them as well.

Incremental deployment will be the preferred method of deploying this technology. However, even for those customers who are moving and considering a greenfield deployment, the incremental migration remains a smart, viable approach.

For example, a company might plan on moving into a new building eight months from now. If this company wants to deploy IP telephony at the new building, the time to begin deploying IPT should, in fact, begin right now. Before it makes the physical move to a new building, it has the opportunity to begin deploying in small pockets, introducing their users (and more importantly, its support organizations) to the technology. This gives its support groups time to learn the technologies and the potential impact on a network in a real-life environment. When the time comes to move, the company will have *real-life* experience and competency about how to support IP telephony technologies in its own environment. It is now real understanding, based on practice.

## Seeing Beyond the PBX

So, in the end, because this is more than a PBX, decision-makers inside companies need to think differently when considering IP telephony. To take full advantage of this technology, you must embrace not only the similarities to the PBX but the vast differences as well. It is the differences that allow companies to truly impact how they conduct business, and that is the focus of the next chapter.

# CHAPTER 5

# FOCUSING ON THE FEW

In the mid 1980s, while I was with Xerox Business Systems, I was introduced to the concept of the *vital few*. The vital few are those three to five initiatives that an organization counts on for success. Every successful company, whether it calls it this or not, focuses on a vital few initiatives, and firm, nonsubjective metrics are in place to measure how well the company is doing with the specific initiatives it has determined to be most critical to its success.

Although different companies might call it by a different name, the concept of the vital few is familiar to many business leaders. This concept is extremely important to the discussion of convergence and IP telephony because impacting those vital few initiatives in an organization is the final, and in the end, most important success metric for a convergence movement.

After an organization has deployed IP telephony, the question on everyone's minds is not going to be: Did it work? The burning question is going to be: *Was it worth it?* The most successful IPT application discovery sessions that lead to business-impacting solutions have come about from a developer being fully aware of the company messages that often are in plain sight. Posters on walls in offices, company newsletter articles, even slogans on business cards often can tell a lot about what is important to a company. These items often give a glimpse into how the vital few of that organization is communicated internally.

The success of a convergence project can be boiled down to seven key questions. These key questions might change somewhat for different sectors (secondary education, for example), but in any for-profit organization, these are the business drivers the company cares about most, and the initiatives that *drive the company to invest in technology.*

Make no mistake, IP telephony is an investment—in time, resources, and money. The return on this investment is going to be critical, and that topic is covered in Chapter 6, "A Different View of ROI." For now, however, put aside the *return* on investment, and consider the *reason* for the investment in the first place. Let's determine how IP telephony can impact this short list of things that a company truly cares about.

In discussions with customers who have deployed IPT or are in the midst of deployments, the following questions are commonly asked:

- How can my company generate more revenue?
- How can we bring products to market faster?
- How can we better cut and control costs?
- How can we better satisfy our customers?
- How can we better satisfy our employees?
- How can we make our employees more productive?
- How can we clearly differentiate ourselves from our competitors?

In planning an IPT deployment, the most important consideration is whether your investment in IP telephony will significantly impact these questions. As with any technology, companies should look to IPT to help boost revenue, control costs, drive employee productivity, and satisfy customers, partners, and suppliers.

This is why much of the first four chapters of this book are dedicated to describing what IP telephony is, and what it is not. The goal for IPT is not just to make phone calls, but to enhance your business processes and make your business better. Identifying the vital few for your organization is an effective method to establish measurements, or metrics, for this evaluation. It removes the subjective nature and ensures that your company is basing success on hard, cold facts.

Many companies that have deployed IP telephony haven't seen any change in revenue, or cost controls, or customer satisfaction. Their employees are no more productive than before they started. Why? How can a company make such a significant investment, bring in such a powerful technology, yet achieve so little impact on those vital few things it cares about most?

As is often the case, the answer is simple: The technology did not impact those vital few elements because that was not the goal of the deployment.

| NOTE | Impacting the vital few initiatives that a company relies on for success should be the goal of any project—especially a convergence project. As with other technology deployments, you get what you plan for. |
| --- | --- |

In fact, for too many companies, the vital few isn't even on the radar screen when they look at this technology. That is a shame, because increasingly, when all is said and done, those companies will be asking themselves, "Why did we do this?"

This type of discussion is consistent with what companies think about when they are investigating technologies for their call centers. Call Center/Contact Center technologies have always been deployed with revenue generation and/or customer support and satisfaction in mind. Those were the exact purposes for the creation of those departments and their associated technologies.

However, when most companies deploy their new phone system, they aren't thinking about revenue generation, customer satisfaction, employee satisfaction, competitive differentiation, or any of the other initiatives they might have in place. Instead, they think about the number of features they have to retain, and how they will train their users. Employee productivity is generally the one vital few initiative addressed by a PBX. Certainly, companies look to get the best deal when procuring a new PBX, but even then, the cost savings are usually limited to the telecom department budget.

So, if the goal of an IPT deployment is to deploy a new kind of telephone and to continue making phone calls just as before with the same feature set, that is the result a company achieves.

Nothing is necessarily wrong with this thinking because phone calls are important. Voice communications remain the foundation of communications within many organizations.

If, however, the goal is to impact one of the critical business processes of that organization, and a plan is developed to do so, then *that* is the result.

The key to success is twofold:

- Develop a strategic and business-impacting reason for deploying IP telephony.

- Develop sound, objective metrics to measure the success of the deployment.

It's not enough to set an objective for revenue gains. Companies must set specific measurable targets:

- How much increase in revenue is expected from this deployment?

- What new relationships with new clients did this project help develop?

- How much of an increase in customer satisfaction is expected from this project?

- How many additional phone calls did this allow sales reps to make (instead of simply looking for productivity enhancements in general)?

- How much cost was recovered from specific business processes because of this new application?

These examples of key initiatives could be considered important to organizations. They impact compensation, career growth, and whether or not a company should hire, maintain status quo, or reduce their workforce. The extent to which a company comprehends the potential impact that this technology might have is vital to the success of a deployment.

Chapter 2, "Wait a Minute...My Phone System Works Just Fine..." briefly introduced the Southwest Airlines model for efficiently running an airline. Now, although this analogy might seem to be a stretch, suppose Southwest Airlines was the first airline company in the world. In this example, this means that there are no airlines, and therefore, air travel as a means of public transportation does not exist.

In this analogy, Southwest, as the world's first airline company, has just ordered its first fleet of aircraft. The Boeing jet comes rolling up to Gate 1 at Love Field in Dallas, Texas, ready for the inaugural flight to San Antonio. Up to this point, the only mode of travel between Dallas and San Antonio has been by car, bus, or train. The passengers are excited about the idea of flying, getting there in one hour instead of five, and seeing clouds from above rather than below. These ideas are the motivators for these passengers, and the reason Southwest invested in jet technology.

So the moment of truth arrives. The plane backs away from the gate, rolls down the runway, makes a quick right turn at Mockingbird Road, rolls for an additional couple of miles until it gets to I-35. At this point, the plane turns south and then, incredibly, proceeds to roll down I-35 for the five-hour drive to San Antonio.

This extreme example hopefully makes its point:

- Did Southwest make a smart investment? Sure.

- Did the investment work? Technically, yes. It got passengers from point A to point B.

- Did it maximize its investment? Certainly not.

This technology was designed to fly. It was designed to differentiate Southwest from the other current forms of public transportation. It was designed to rapidly speed up travel by an order of magnitude from cars, buses, and trains. Did it do any of these things? No, but technically it worked, because passengers did, in fact, arrive safely in San Antonio.

Jets and airplanes are not designed to just get people from one place to another. They are designed to fly at speeds ground transportation cannot approach, and therefore provide a different value proposition to the end user (in this case, a passenger).

In the same manner, IP telephony is not designed just to make phone calls. It is designed to interoperate with other network applications and introduce new applications that impact the key initiatives companies put into action. Deploying IPT without new applications is like buying a jet and driving it on the highway.

# Understanding the Value Proposition

The first objective of organizations investigating IP telephony should be to identify those specific areas in their own businesses that can be measurably improved because of new applications and new clients enabled by this technology.

If the idea that running applications on corporate phones can improve business seems far-fetched, consider the cellular market for a moment. Just over a decade ago, the notion that everyone would have a cell phone was so preposterous that you would have been laughed out of a meeting had you suggested the type of market acceptance enjoyed by cellular technologies today.

Furthermore, the cell phone has already evolved before our eyes. It is not uncommon to see consumers picking up e-mail, checking favorite websites, instant messaging friends, or even playing games on their cell phones. All this is possible because of new applications aimed at that particular device. So it shall be with IP phones and IP telephony. As businesses begin to see the IP phone as an intelligent client, they can begin to realize the potential for adding new capabilities and impacting business processes.

## Cheap Phone Versus Intelligent Client

Customers adopting new IP phones running new network-based applications are finding that this is not consistent with the "cheaper is best" philosophy that has thrived in the past 20 years of PBX technology. Enabling a telephone to connect directly to an IP network, interface with network applications, and be managed by network resources requires additional technology and capabilities that current digital phones do not possess. The incremental costs added to IP phones giving them these capabilities are offset only if the company deploying them utilizes them to their fullest extent.

## Features Versus Capabilities

As previously noted, most companies focus on features during their procurement of phone systems. They focus on the features they currently have, and work to ensure they don't lose any functionality.

Moving forward, companies looking at IP telephony are increasingly moving the focus away from "what features I have" to "what capabilities I do not have." More specifically, "what are those new capabilities that might not exist yet, but can be developed" that will positively impact their business, their key initiatives, and especially their vital few.

For law firms, the focus is increasingly moving away from using forced authorization codes to validate users, and moving towards new applications that use the concept of forced authorization codes to simplify and increase the accuracy of the billing process—a key business goal for the legal industry.

For a pharmaceutical company, the focus is moving away from simply having distribution groups within voice-messaging platforms to true collaborative applications bringing together voice, video, and data to more effectively distribute analysis of test results from clinical trials—a key business goal for the pharmaceutical industry.

In secondary schools, the focus is moving away from simply restricting calls from coming into the classroom during specific hours, and moving to enhance the security of the school campus by enabling one-touch recording, tracking, and online reporting to police authorities of threatening phone calls, which is increasingly a key business goal for schools today.

So, the focus shifts, the expectations increase, and technologies have a more fundamental impact on businesses than ever before—when that is the *goal* for the organization.

## A Different Buying Process

This fundamental shift in expectations is causing an important and beneficial change in the buying process for companies. This is not going to be a slam dunk for manufacturers and providers of these convergence solutions. This technology is encouraging vendors, partners, and manufacturers to leave the quick sale mentality and adopt a more consultative approach to jointly identify business needs and potential solutions with their customers. More people have to be involved in identifying business requirements for a company with this technology.

It also means that companies must quickly develop a deeper trust with specific vendors and partners, because they aren't going to open up and share their business with just anyone. True, many of the key initiatives they have in place might be fairly public knowledge. As previously mentioned, much of this is evident if you walk through their halls, view their collateral materials, or read their annual reports.

However, the internal business processes that are inherently affecting and affected by these initiatives are not so evident, and this information is shared only with trusted partners. It is not broadcast during bid meetings, it usually isn't contained in a request for proposal (RFP).

Yet without the partner having this important information, the desired state for the customer likely remains unrealized. Without this new focus, without sharing of business initiatives and expectations, the customer ends up with an IP-PBX—a new telephone system that has just been moved to a new home—but one that, again, doesn't significantly impact the vital few.

Partners who adopt a consultative approach are able to provide a deployment that is tailored to the needs of the business. Therefore, the success of the technology deployment is determined by the extent to which the partner providing the technology and solutions understands the customer's key initiatives, the key business processes that support those initiatives, and the people that are integral to these processes.

After a key business process is fully understood, then an understanding of the various workgroups and work processes that are a part of that key business process must occur. Also, an assessment of the applications, documents, and technology features that are critical to the work process is required.

At this point, a partner has enough information to potentially develop a new application that can impact a business initiative.

Figure 5-1 shows the aspects of the business that a partner must understand to be effective. During a traditional TDM/PBX project, the focus is immediately drawn to the bottom of this diagram; specifically, the features. As explained previously, retaining existing features is one of the main priorities for a new telephone system deployment.

However, an understanding of features, or even applications, does not translate into business impact unless the provider/developer understands the work process and business processes affected. Therefore, a good IP telephony implementation begins at the top, with an understanding of key initiatives in place for the company, and those key business processes that are impacted.

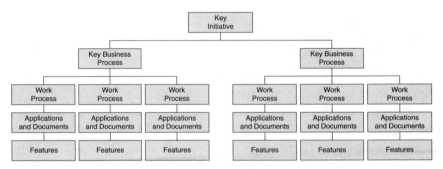

*Figure 5-1* *Understanding the Business Is the Key to Convergence*

# Sample Business Cases

The model in Figure 5-1 can identify business needs and turn that knowledge into a new type of application that addresses specific requirements. This model can be applied to six different sectors:

- Hospitality
- Secondary education
- Higher education
- Retail
- Health care
- Finance

## Hospitality/Hotels

Hotels have been relatively slow to adopt IP telephony. This industry is heavily focused on costs—ironically, cost containment is turning into one of the major initiatives that is causing this industry to investigate IPT. Initially, however, the thinking was as follows:

"We need to contain our costs. Our phones work just fine. Our guests are not asking for smarter phones, but looking for entertainment and tools to help them conduct business while traveling. We don't need new voice technologies at this time, we just need more 'heads on beds.'"

This thought process dominated most decision makers in the hospitality industry when they were initially introduced to IP telephony. However, as the potential for new types of applications continues to surface, leaders in these organizations are beginning to align their expectations with how IPT can significantly impact their specific initiatives. One initiative, for example, pertains to room service.

Room service is a key business process in many full-service hotels because it generates revenue for the hotel and enhances customer satisfaction by providing a convenient service to clients. As in other industries, the traditional sources of revenue are changing. In recent years, for example, the prevalence of cell phones has dramatically reduced the revenues that hotels earn from long-distance calls made by guests. Hotels are looking for new ways to increase their revenues and control costs. Looking specifically at the work process involved for providing in-room breakfast service, some clear opportunities for business impact become evident.

The menu, for example, represents an investment in design, printing, and perhaps even translation services. As such, the menu is part of the cost of sales that a hotel incurs to offer room service. In an IP telephony business assessment, the goal is to find applications and/or documents that can be enhanced.

The menu is usually multicolored, double-sided, and printed on heavy stock paper. It often has a special perforation that allows it to hang on a doorknob. This menu, depending on its complexity, can easily be $0.75 to $1.25 per document, and the hotel provides one in every room, every night.

Now, consider the process itself. George checks into his room late at night and wants to order breakfast for the morning. He makes his selection on the menu, and hangs the menu outside his door. Later in the night, someone comes by and retrieves this document. This is labor to the hotel. The employee takes the document downstairs into the kitchen, where someone enters the information into a computer system. This, too, is labor cost to the hotel.

Yet another consideration remains. These menus have a reminder to hang the document on the door by midnight, suggesting that at some point, this process is cut off. In other words, potential revenue is cut off. In the case of someone who is arriving on a late-night flight and checking-in at the hotel too late to set up breakfast, a potential loss of room service revenue exists for the hotel.

Figure 5-2 shows the relationship between the initiative, key business process, work process, application/document, and feature for this opportunity.

*Figure 5-2* *Hospitality Business Opportunity*

Up to this point, all these have been considered fixed and necessary costs for the breakfast room service. The question is, can IP telephony, or more specifically, IP telephony applications, impact this process? Can any costs from this process be reduced through convergence? The answer is yes.

Figure 5-3 depicts a typical application being deployed in hotel rooms because of IP telephony. This type of application is currently provided by applications development organizations, such as Calence, Percipia, and Norstan.

This hospitality application is designed for IP phones in hotel rooms. It presents a myriad of opportunities for customer service, revenue generation, and employee productivity for hotel staff. It is made possible by placing a more intelligent device in hotel rooms.

*Figure 5-3* *Room Service as an Application for Hospitality*

In this example, a guest in the hotel would press 3 on the phone keypad to launch the breakfast menu. Everything contained in the menu document can be presented on the screen of this IP phone—and more. In fact, additional items can now be offered to increase the variety to the guest. Now that it is no longer printed, the menu can change weekly, monthly, or seasonally, which adds flexibility and convenience while eliminating printing expenses.

In addition, as guests make their selections, their entries are automatically updating the application in the kitchen. This eliminates the need for hotel staff to walk the hallways retrieving menus, and enter the information manually. Again, cost savings from a labor perspective.

Additionally, the guest can pick up the phone and be connected to the hotel kitchen, or automatically leave a voice message that can be electronically appended to the order. For example, the menu might offer milk, but the traveler could pick up the phone and request chocolate milk. In the kitchen, when the order is pulled up for processing, not only does the staff see the order in the computer, but a flashing phone icon indicates that a voice message request is attached to this order.

Finally, because this application is running on the phone, the guest can place this order as early or as late as they want. The cut-off period can be virtually eliminated, as long as there is enough time to process and cook the order, because it is delivered immediately into the kitchen application. The potential for revenue is never turned off.

With IP telephony, the hotel benefits from printing savings, labor savings, and extended hours for revenue. These are all critical impact points in the room-service business process designed to make the revenue collected more profitable for the hotel. The annual savings for a single hotel can be in the tens or hundreds of thousands of dollars—and this is just one application.

Other applications offer the potential for revenue generation by enabling on-screen advertising to area entertainment, and the potential for enhanced productivity by allowing hotel staff to place orders for missing items, or to update room status visually on the phone. Finally, because many of the IP phones available today have an integrated, built-in Ethernet switch, the interface for high-speed Internet access is now built right into the phone, saving the expense of another form of connectivity and duplicate cabling.

These are some of the possibilities that the hospitality industry is starting to deploy. The key was the realization that this is more than just a phone. When the industry's expectations increased, the discussion with its vendors and partners moved away from phone features to impacting business initiatives for the hotel.

# K–12 Education

Schools are among the earliest adopters of IP telephony, and this sector continues to raise the bar in terms of business-impacting applications. Although this might be a bit surprising, it makes sense considering the type of organization a school actually is:

- A school district is a safe haven where parents send their children for up to eight hours a day during the business week. Of course, children receive an education, but they also are supposed to be in a secure environment. A high emphasis is placed on security. Events in recent years have only heightened this as a priority.

- A school district is a public transportation system. It provides a scheduled pick up and delivery of "customers"; in this case, children.

- A school district is a multifranchised restaurant. *Each* school in the district has a cafeteria that provides two meals a day for its students.

- Finally, schools must hire and retain excellent college-educated professionals to educate children, and do all this based on taxes raised and diminishing government budgets.

Thinking of a school in this context, it is an organization with a number of challenges most people have never considered. A transportation company has its own challenges. A restaurant has its own issues to deal with. Combine these two into a single entity, add the need for a high level of security, the education factor and diminishing budgets, and you have an organization with significant challenges.

As a result of these challenges, a wealth of new applications exists that are geared toward helping schools navigate through the daily issues presented to them. New applications can provide better ways to do the following:

- Notify parents and teachers if buses are running late
- Ensure that progress reports end up in the possession of parents
- Help parents and teachers communicate
- Control student loitering in the halls

IP telephony can address all these issues, and is doing so in many schools today. It begins with those schools seeing IPT as more than just a phone system.

The electronic hall pass, which was detailed in Chapter 4, "If This Isn't a PBX, What Is It?," helps address the issue of student loitering. However, security is increasingly becoming a major initiative for public schools, and they are looking at IP telephony solutions as a means of enhancing security. One example of school security concerns is the bomb threat.

The bomb threat is a definite reality for public schools today. Two years ago, a fairly affluent school district in north Texas closed two weeks early for the summer because of the number of bomb threats they were receiving. School officials suspect that many of these threats were ruses from students to force the school to close. Yet, because of recent tragic events involving students, schools can no longer assume that these calls were merely student pranks.

How can IP telephony help schools deal with this issue? Let's take the example of Mrs. Wright, a high-school history teacher in a suburban school district. The district recently rolled out IP telephony to the classrooms, either in the form of new IP phones on the teachers' desks, or in the form of IP SoftPhone software running on their desktop PC. The teachers are excited because they finally have the ability to make and place calls from the classroom. In reality, they have much more.

A call comes in during Mrs. Wright's free period. During regular teaching hours, the blocking application would not let any calls come through except from the main office, unless an emergency occurs in another classroom. In that case, the teacher calling Mrs. Wright could enter an emergency override that would supercede the traditional time-of-day blocking feature available for most classroom environments.

Mrs. Wright answers the phone. It immediately becomes clear that the call is of a threatening nature. She presses a button on the phone (or an icon on her PC SoftPhone application), and the following occurs:

- The call is recorded. The call is stored as a .wav file on a server, and automatically filed in a security folder.

- The application grabs the ANI/calling party information. If this information was passed from the central office, this number is now captured and available.

- The application also grabs the DNIS/called number information, which captures whom was called.

- Both of these pieces of information are attached to an alert, which immediately goes to the IP phones and PC applications running in the school office, and to the administration building.

- If the school district has chosen to do so, a dedicated VPN link into the local police station is in place. The application immediately sends an alert, with the called party and calling party information sent to the police desk.

- Now, the police have an audio and visual notification of a security situation at the school. If the school has extended even a single IP phone from its network into the police department, the police can, at the touch of a button, conference in on the conversation while it is still taking place.

- Because the police, via an IP phone, are listening in, they can, from their desktop or IP phone, send an instant message to Mrs. Wright at the school, coaching her through the call and requesting she keep the caller on the phone.

- The police can use their public databases to determine the location of the telephone placing the call and immediately route a patrol car to the location, again, while the call is still taking place.

Notice that all this is occurring simply because Mrs. Wright has been trained during summer security workshops to press a single button/icon on the phone in the event of an emergency, and within seconds, all the previous activities are in place, taking action.

Because of the security issues facing schools today and the expectations of parents that their children will be safe, this type of application is not just interesting, but could become commonplace in schools in the coming years. This takes advantage of the IP nature of an IPT solution, extending devices across networks, interconnecting networks using VPN capabilities, saving voice recordings on the network, and it is available to any client on the network. These types of capabilities are now being comprehended by school officials.

Additional potential for this technology exists when intelligent IP clients—whether phones or workstations—are deployed in classrooms with voice/telephony capabilities. Consider a bus that has broken down in the transportation garage. The school is scrambling for another bus, and a means of notifying parents that the bus will be late. A straightforward application can be developed that allows school officials to look up a bus number, and at the press of a button, the application does the following:

- Asks the school official to record a voice message explaining the situation
- Captures the names of every student on the bus that has broken down
- Captures the students' home phone numbers from their profiles
- Creates an autodial list containing these phone numbers
- Begins calling each student's home, and delivers the message recorded by the school official

With this application, families are immediately alerted that the bus is running late and have the option of making alternate plans for getting their children to school. Further, when contact is made with the parent, the application can ask the parent to press 1 if they are bringing their child, or to press 2 if the child will still wait for the bus. In this way, the school is immediately notified if certain children do not need to be picked up, which could enable the bus to regain some of the time that has been lost.

Because the school is a transportation company as well as an education facility, this type of application is now extremely appealing to them. Consider schools in the Midwest or on the East Coast, where winter weather could play havoc with schedules. This becomes a tool at their disposal to help them manage through situations like this.

Other applications take advantage of the alerting features of IP telephony. Not only can applications provide alerts based on activities or logical events, but physical events as well. Schools are now placing nondescript, wireless smoke detectors in restrooms. These devices send a message to a wireless receiver when smoke is detected. The wireless receiver transmits a subsequent message to an IPT application that sends a visual and audible alarm to the IP phones in either room adjacent to the restroom, notifying the teachers in those rooms that a student is likely smoking in the restroom.

Another example of an IPT application in schools is one geared toward special schools that are established for students with behavior issues. In some of these schools, teachers wear a necklace with a panic button that can be depressed when they are faced with a dangerous or challenging situation. The depressed panic button sends a signal to a wireless receiver, which subsequently transmits a message to an IPT application that visually and audibly alerts security or office personnel of the situation.

A key point to remember, however, is that many of these business-impacting applications are not currently sitting on the shelf somewhere, waiting for a buyer. These applications are the product of application workshops with school officials, where they discuss their specific requirements with a developer who understands the convergence model. The developer then creates and deploys these applications, customized to the school's requirements. Some applications might be pre-existing, but many could be developed in conjunction with school officials.

These are just a few of the examples of business-impacting applications that are being used and/or discussed by school officials. Figure 5-4 shows a sample screen from Sentinel, a developer that has successfully deployed IP telephony applications in the Kindergarten through grade 12 (K–12) market.

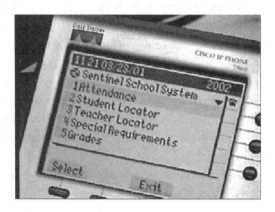

*Figure 5-4* *K–12 Applications from Sentinel*

## Higher Education

Along with the K–12 market, the higher education market has been among the early adopters of IP telephony solutions. Colleges were among the first sectors to take advantage of the advertising capabilities of IPT, although in most cases, this is referred to as *corporate sponsorships*. The idea is to use the screen of the IP phone as a means of generating revenue by selling advertising space or time to other companies.

For colleges, this has been as simple as a Pizza Hut ad rolling across the screen of IP phones in the student dormitories, as shown in Figure 5-5. This is a natural advertising opportunity in the dorm because it reaches the market that fast-food chains are trying to reach on the college campus: the student who is tired of eating at the college cafeteria. Advertising is a means of recapturing some of the lost revenue when students take their eating dollars elsewhere. New streams of revenue, and new cost controls, are two of the primary motivators for colleges and universities that might be considering deploying IP telephony.

***Figure 5-5*** *Sample of a Pizza Hut Ad in a Student Dorm Room*

The opportunities for higher education institutions don't stop here, however. In some respects, this market faces similar challenges as the hospitality market. Just as the cell phone has been a major source of revenue loss for the hotel, so has it been for colleges and universities. Now, although most students in dorm rooms still choose to have a phone in their rooms, the option of paying for long-distance service versus placing phone calls on their cell phones often turns into a lost revenue opportunity for the university.

Universities are looking for additional revenue-producing opportunities. As they learn more about the potential of IP telephony, they are beginning to search for new, advanced applications that can help attain these fiscal initiatives. Ironically, many students are finding that an IP phone in the dorm room is an easier, more friendly, and less intimidating device than the laptop personal computer that the students have either brought with them or that have been provided by the university.

On the surface, this sounds more than a bit odd. It just doesn't seem possible that this generation of students would be intimidated by a computer. The idea that these same young person who surf the web, download music, have multiple e-mail addresses, and use instant messaging to communicate with friends and family around the world could have problems with a laptop is, indeed, far-fetched. However, these students don't necessarily have problems with their laptops (hardware) as much as they do the university applications on the network (software). I found this to be true when I enrolled my 18-year-old "whiz kid" daughter into Trinity University for her freshman year.

We moved her into her dorm room the weekend before school started. The instructions for hooking up her computer to the network were waiting for her on her desk in her room. I sat back and watched, somewhat amused, as this young computer prodigy sat with a confused look on her face. She called the dormitory assistant, who instructed us to go to the next building where a computer help desk had been set up. As we approached the building, we saw the bad news waiting for us. The length of the line we were getting ready to stand in was something I won't forget.

It struck me as odd that all these young people would be having so many computer problems. When we finally sat down with an IS volunteer, I took the opportunity to investigate. The volunteer informed us that this, in fact, was quite normal. The same students who spent so much of their time on the Internet in high school were unprepared for the networking environment presented to them at the university. Understanding how to download and update templates, and download software other than music-sharing programs was quite a task for these young adults. Setting up printers and setting up Outlook parameters for the university e-mail system were all new experiences for the freshmen.

I realized then that touch-of-a-button applications—ones that did not need to be loaded on a laptop (or a phone)—that could help students see grades, buy books, or order tickets would be popular with students and with the university. Having access to these types of applications and services without having to load anything on their laptops would be a significant benefit of IP telephony. Now, with phone-based applications that enable instant messaging and access to Internet sites, this is becoming a reality.

## Retail

Although there is now significant movement in the retail industry, this has been one of the slower markets to adopt IP telephony, at least at the store level. At various regional and/or headquarter locations, the value proposition from the distributed nature of IPT is as relevant in this industry as in any other. However, for this discussion, the focus is limited to the actual stores.

In focusing on stores, it is helpful to expand the definition of retail. Retail, as far as this discussion is concerned, includes any storefront that sells products and/or services, which would include traditional retail shopping, specialty stores, grocery stores, drug stores, and gas stations.

In each of these cases, the value proposition for IP telephony applications usually focus on enhanced, faster communications, updates, and cost controls. Generally, these markets are margin driven, so any means of cutting and controlling costs on an ongoing basis is good news—obviously good news for any company, but also necessary for survival in these markets.

Chapter 4 described how one of the major benefits of IP telephony was the ability to help drive down company costs in various business processes, beyond the maintenance of the PBX. Nowhere is this more evident than in the retail industry. From the costs for supporting the help desk to payroll/timecard costs, new IPT applications can have a significant impact on these costs. With the exception of K—12 schools, clearly the most imaginative applications are being developed in the retail market.

Chapter 6, "A Different View of ROI," explains how toll charges can be dramatically reduced by IP telephony without necessarily passing voice traffic over the IP network. In one example, only data commands traverse the network, and therefore bandwidth impact is minimal.

Another type of application could be called "timecard maintenance." Initially, this sounds like a fairly simple application, but it can have an incredibly far-reaching impact.

Timecard entry on an IP phone is a new way to track employee work hours. The ongoing costs of punch cards and punch machines can be eliminated. The real value, however, lies in automating and electronically tracking the employee clocking-in/clocking-out process. This means that application parameters can be set to detect when a person *should* have clocked out, but hasn't. An alert can then be sent to that person's manager, either via IP phone, cell phone, or pager, etc.

For example, it is now 5:05 P.M. and seven employees who should be off the clock have yet to punch out. The application detects this, alerts management, who can then take action. With this application, unplanned and/or unauthorized overtime payments are avoided, which helps the company's bottom line.

Another issue that can be tackled by such an application is fraudulent reporting of hours. For example, the same timecard maintenance application can be expanded to provide additional services to the employee. When an employee enters their employee ID and a personal identification number (PIN), the menu could provide the following options:

- Clock in
- Clock out
- Last pay stub
- Year-to-date earnings

In reality, most employees won't necessarily want to check their last pay stub or their year-to-date earnings, but having these options as part of the time clocking application isn't necessarily limited to employee benefit alone. By adding this personal and private information, the company has just made it a bit more difficult for John, who is 30 minutes away from the store and running late, to call his buddy Mark and have Mark clock him in. Now, in order for Mark to clock John in, John must share his employee ID and PIN with Mark, which gives Mark access to John's personal information. This provides an electronic time clock and an imaginative way to deal with fraudulent reporting, all enabled by a convergence application.

These are just two examples of what is occurring in the retail space. NetCom Systems recently rolled out an IP dial-out application to a large, national energy company. According to Alok Jain, director of Applications Development, the long-term opportunity for this company is to place intelligent voice/data terminals at each of this company's gas stations, whereby station managers can receive corporate-initiated price changes in seconds, visually on their workstation, with a voice message attached to the price change. An example, in this case, of revenue-impacting applications.

## Health Care

In March of 2002, Cisco Systems held their second applications Expo/Bake-Off for application developers to show the market the new services and applications available for IP telephony customers. The winner of this event was Calence, a Cisco certified partner and applications developer. The application Calence designed had standing-room only crowds for each demonstration, and truly opened the eyes of virtually everyone there — customer, vendor, and partner alike.

The application was a voice-activated prescription program aimed at the medical and pharmaceutical markets. It allowed a doctor, for example, to issue voice commands to a phone-based application, and the application would respond with appropriate prescription types, dosages, etc.

Take this to the next logical step: The doctor, after issuing the prescription verbally, scans the prescription card on an IP phone with a card reader and a list of nearby pharmacies is displayed on the phone. The doctor then issues a command to send the prescription request to the patient's pharmacy of choice. Or, this feature could be restricted to the hospital's own pharmacy to promote more use of their own facility (and generating more revenue for the hospital).

Cari c'deBaca, a program manager for application developers at Cisco Systems, is one of the most visionary "thought leaders" I have met in the convergence space. Having been with Selsius Systems from the beginning, and having the distinction of installing the industry's first true, native IP telephony system into a production environment in 1997, she has had plenty of time to watch and impact this emerging industry.

Cari often speaks to business leaders interested in convergence about "having a conversation with your data." Not keystrokes. Conversation.

For doctors and nurses, this is the ultimate in voice technologies because it allows them to communicate with computers the way they truly prefer; that is, by issuing voice commands and receiving visual data responses. It opens the door for truly revolutionary tools to help them save lives. Voice-activated prescriptions are just the proverbial tip of the iceberg for this industry.

Voice commands to invoke a video conference to bring in another doctor during surgeries, to open collaborative sessions with colleagues, to access test results while making hospital rounds—these are the future of IP telephony in the health care market.

Figure 5-6 shows a wireless tablet, one of the wireless clients that many believe could become a common device in the medical field in the coming years. This tablet can act as a monitor in a docked environment, or, when the doctor or nurse walks the hospital floors, can be removed from the docking station and used as a full-functioning wireless client with access to all data resources, as well as wireless voice/telephony capabilities. The new breed of IP telephony applications for this client might focus on voice-activated commands that enable the user to interact more easily with voice, video, data, and collaborative applications, because constantly stopping to enter keyboard commands is not productive.

The continuing emergence of the Health Insurance Portability and Accountability Act (HIPAA) provides standards as well as opportunities for new application development. This health care reform law was passed by the U.S. Congress in 1996 and became law in 2001. It is designed to improve the efficiency and effectiveness of the health care system, help providers access patient's health care information, standardize the way the information is handled, and ensure that patient health information remains strictly confidential.

***Figure 5-6*** *Wireless Tablet Tool for Doctors and Nurses, with Integrated Soft-Phone Client*

Standards for effective, yet secure, sharing of patient and health care information using new technologies could play an important role for hospitals as they move towards compliance with these new standards.

## Banking and Finance

Part of the challenge with the banking and finance industry lies in the realization that more than any other vertical market, banking and finance institutions have allowed (in fact, encouraged) the focus on their IP telephony deployments to be squarely on their existing feature set. Although other industries have coped with IPT's initial limited feature set while developing new capabilities, the banking and finance industry for the most part, has dug in and refused to budge until such time as their existing features are available with IP telephony.

This is not an indictment against this industry, but a viewpoint as to why more applications have not surfaced in this market. The reason is simply because application development has not been the focus. The focus has been on recreating the existing feature set. As this focus changes and the market continues to mature, the same type of outside-the-box thinking should occur in this market as has been seen in others.

This is already starting, as evidenced by some of the newer experiences partners are now having with large financial institutions. At the time of this writing, at least one large institution is looking to pilot IP telephony technologies as an integrated component of their automatic teller machines (ATMs). Part of the thought process is to create an environment where customers using ATMs and running into any kind of difficulty could, at the touch of a button, have either voice or voice/video sessions invoked with a representative at the bank's call center. The video angle is being investigated as it lends itself to the security aspects of the solution.

For example, Sam Johnson is having problems with his account at a neighborhood ATM. He invokes a session with a bank representative. At this point, how does the representative know this is actually Sam, and not someone who has stolen Sam's card? So, the video component is critical, as it allows the bank representative to visually verify the identity of the customer. The video image seen by the bank representative can be compared with a digital image captured by the bank when Sam was issued his card, or when he opened his account. This capability exists within the framework of IP telephony today, and is only now being considered by financial institutions.

## Security

Our office in Dallas is on the first floor, in the front of a relatively new building. Usually, about 15 of us are working in the office, and sometimes even fewer than that because of travel. Construction is still going on in the building, and new companies are moving in and making change requests. This means strangers occasionally make their way into our office. We are placing sensors on the front and back doors so that when either door is opened, the sensor indicates as such, and can send a visual alert to every IP phone in the office. We don't want an alert sent to our PC because, depending on the time of day, our PC might not be turned on, and also because we don't want to have yet another application barging in on PC-based applications already running.

With this application, everyone in the office will be alerted if someone enters. The plan is to invoke this application after 4:30 in the afternoon. Additionally, there is a plan to place a video camera at the front desk, so that when the application sends an alert to the IP phone, it can also send a quick video feed of whomever came in. Again, this was our own determination of how to secure our premises. These types of applications could become commonplace in the coming years.

So, even though a PC might be at the desktop, a phone-based application might make sense on a case-by-case basis. Remember, the goal is not to deploy more of the same, but to look for new ways to impact business. Beginning with this "desired state" is the key.

# Right Around the Corner...

This chapter concludes with the realization that sophisticated users, who always create markets, are now questioning why their laptops, Palm Pilots, cell phones, and other PDAs can be so intelligent, yet their work phone remains "dumbed down." They question the fact that what is arguably the most important device in the work environment remains shielded from technology advancements. More than anything else, it is this shift in the expectations of the sophisticated user that will launch the applications of the future for the new phones and voice clients of the workplace.

The voice-activated prescription handling application for IP phones that won Cisco Systems 2002 Applications Expo surprised even the original Selsius Systems engineers responsible for developing IP telephony technologies. None of us saw that coming, and anticipation is high for future Expo/Bake-Off events to see what new developments are brought to light. This is the nature of the evolvement of Internet technologies, and it is being driven down to business phones in the workplace.

Sophisticated users might find opportunities where an application running on the phone makes more sense "for that time" and "for that particular user." They might find critical documents that still exist in paper form and are an integral part of key business processes in their organization, and ask, "Why are these documents still in paper form? Why haven't we migrated them to electronic documents? Wouldn't it make more sense for these documents to be accessed or invoked by/from a phone?"

These sophisticated users will determine when it makes sense to link data with a phone call. They won't be limited to thinking about phones when they think of voice. They will ask for, and eventually demand, wireless voice capabilities on their wireless clients, and have voice seamlessly interact with their data applications on these clients. The wireless tablet is an example of this, with soft-clients and wireless technologies for handling voice calls.

Color capabilities are just around the corner from many manufacturers of IP phones. Color is going to make the IP phone client far more attractive and accessible for users and application developers who are accustomed to high-resolution screens and use of color in their applications. Touch-screen capabilities are already here, as seen with Norstan's Boss-Admin suite of soft-clients for desktops, laptops, PDAs, and wireless tablets. Manufacturers adding Java support to the XML/HTML phones of today will open the doors for more developers with even greater tools.

As noted, not all voice applications run on the phones anyway. Many run in the background on the network, controlling call handling, messaging, and alerting functions. These applications, although not necessarily visual in nature, still have tremendous business impact.

At the end of the day, the discussion comes back to the vital few—that short list of business initiatives that the company *must* address to be successful. This leads to the subject of the next chapter, ROI—the elusive return on investment.

# A DIFFERENT VIEW OF ROI

This discussion on return on investment (ROI) begins with another flashback to my Selsius Systems days. In the summer of 1998, I was embarrassingly, but convincingly introduced into the first aspects of IP telephony ROI. My new office was ready for me to move into, and it was time to pack up and move. At that time, I was a VP for this start-up technology company marketing the benefits of IPT. I spoke to customers and partners continuously about the ease of management, the reduction in moves, adds, and changes (MAC), the benefits of a single cable plant and single drop to the desktop. Yet, when the time came for me to move to a new office, I lapsed into old, familiar territory: I picked up the phone and called our telecom department to arrange to have my phone moved.

The person I called was Cari c'deBaca, who I have mentioned in previous chapters. At that time, Cari was the head of information services (IS) and telecom for Selsius Systems. Cari had a staff of one to handle all the IS and telecommunications requirements for the company.

When I asked what I had to do to move my phone into the new office and get service, I was reminded that this was IP telephony, and I didn't have to ask anyone for help in moving my phone. So, I unplugged my phone, moved to my new office, and plugged the phone back in. Seconds later, I was making phone calls and conducting business.

My lesson with streamlined administration continued later that year in early December when Cisco Systems acquired Selsius Systems. When the time came for all the Selsius employees to move from the Intecom building to the new Cisco offices a few miles north, Cari and her staff gave clear, concise, and detailed instructions on how we, as users, were to handle the move.

"Pack your stuff in the boxes. They will be moved for you. When you get to your new office or cube, plug the phone into the jack, and plug your laptop computer into your phone."

That was the extent of the move. Because we had DHCP servers, we literally could unplug phones and/or laptops, and they would register with the appropriate server and obtain an IP address automatically when they were plugged back into the network.

A year and a half later, when the new Cisco campus opened in Richardson and multiple office buildings were consolidated, we were all old pros. We packed our boxes, went to the new offices, and plugged in.

This might seem simple, but that is the point: Because of the IP-nature of IP telephony, Moves, Adds and Changes (MAC) is simplified. Cabling is simplified. Administration is simplified. Finally, IP telephony looks like other applications, appliances, and clients on the network.

Remember the concept of the "vital few" from Chapter 5, "Focusing on the Few"? Impacting the vital few for an organization changes the entire scope of an ROI discussion. It adds the fiscal impact of improving business processes to the fiscal impact of IPT.

# A Different Approach to ROI

Up to this point, most telephony decisions have been a quick study in procurement. Businesses try to ensure feature retention, get a good price on the digital phones, and keep as many analog phones as possible. The goal is to get into the new investment with as little outlay as possible. The ROI is going to be a lengthy five- to seven-year process. That's the perspective of the traditional world of voice that businesses are moving away from.

IP telephony shrinks the five- to seven-year write-off period by streamlining administration, requiring fewer support resources (or consolidated resources between telecom and IS), cable plant savings, hardware procurement savings, and reduced year-over-year maintenance. These savings can reduce the ROI period to less than two years, and in many cases, less than a year.

The final step in maximizing the potential ROI lies with the deployment of convergence applications that impact targeted business processes within the organization. Impacting those vital few areas takes convergence into the final frontier, the world of cost recovery.

To maximize ROI, the focus for an organization is not on writing off a purchase of a telephone system, but on identifying business initiatives that can be rapidly and cost-effectively addressed by IPT solutions. The goal is to drive rapid financial returns for a business process investment that adds revenue to the bottom line, enables long-term cost containments within business units, or enhances customer satisfaction.

The goal does not end with getting the investment back, but extends into driving permanent cost containments that recover costs from the budget that were previously considered part of the cost of doing business. The example discussed for hotels in Chapter 5 is a good example of this thinking, and is expanded upon later in this chapter. For now, let's begin with the more obvious elements of ROI, and then continue to build the case.

Consider these elements in a discussion of ROI for IP telephony:

- Network costs
- Administrative costs
- Maintenance costs
- The impact of applications on key company initiatives

The following sections examine each of these elements. The impact of applications is shown through examples of deployments in a variety of industries.

# Network Costs

The idea of a single network replacing multiple networks is clearly the first element to be considered when calculating ROI for an IPT deployment. A single network means less equipment, streamlined administration, and less maintenance. All these benefits have a financial impact on the organization. Let's begin with the savings in equipment.

Figure 6-1 shows an enterprise with a headquarters location and a regional office. The PBX is located at the headquarters location, and the voice-mail system is also there. At this location, users with phones access the public network for external calls through trunk cards that are installed in the PBX cabinets. This is the traditional environment for TDM technology.

This environment is duplicated at the regional branch; that is, a PBX, voice-mail system, users with phones, and trunk cards in the PBX for public access.

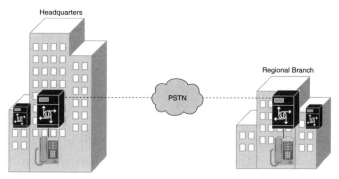

***Figure 6-1*** *The Enterprise Voice Environment, Pre-Convergence*

In this example, the company in question has made duplicate purchases throughout its network. In other words, every location has a phone system. That phone system consists of, at a minimum, a PBX or key system and potentially a voice-mail system as well. So, at each location, the company is paying for

- Voice cabinets
- Voice line cards for desktop devices (phones)
- Voice trunk cards for public access
- CPU equipment for voice call set-up and release
- TDM equipment for transmission control
- Voice mail cabinets
- Trunk facilities to accommodate the transmission of voice sessions between voice mail and the PBX

To this environment, the company now needs to add the data components of the enterprise, as shown in Figure 6-2.

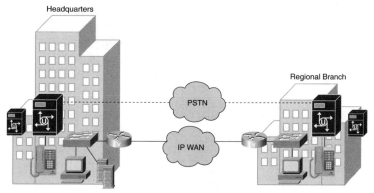

***Figure 6-2*** *The Enterprise Voice and Data Environment, Pre-Convergence*

In addition to the voice equipment, different components have been added that perform a similar function for the data requirements. The data switch provides data port connectivity for the data workstations (PCs, laptops, etc.). In the data environment, the TDM-switching functionality for data is performed by this data switch, which provides the functionality of a line card and TDM switch for the data side of the house. So, now multiple components essentially do similar things, but for different networks.

Notice also the router that is now included in the picture. The router performs the external connectivity for the data environment; i.e., voice trunks provide public connections to the outside environment, and routers provide private, or WAN connections to the outside environment. In the case of data, however, the outside environment is another location of the enterprise that is on the same network. The router extends the boundaries of the network beyond its local limits.

Now, as seen with the enterprise voice network in Figure 6-1, the company must, for the most part, make duplicate purchases throughout the network. Each location requires connectivity points (data switches) and external WAN connectivity to interconnect various locations—in this case, the headquarters and regional office.

Figure 6-3, however, shows a convergence deployment, which means the elimination of a separate voice network. This reduces costs by eliminating a separate PBX, separate voice line cards, trunk cards, TDM switching matrix, and cabling. In Figure 6-3, all these elements are now integrated within the existing IP network. Figure 6-3 shows a single network, handling both voice and data, and video requirements with a single infrastructure of components.

Certainly, some companies might be concerned about fully integrating voice and data onto a single network. In their minds, if they lose the network, they lose both voice and data, which does not happen in a traditional PBX environment. Chapter 7, "Watch That First Step," touches on those activities that can (and should) be initiated to ensure the same level of reliability and availability on a converged network that companies have come to expect from their voice networks.

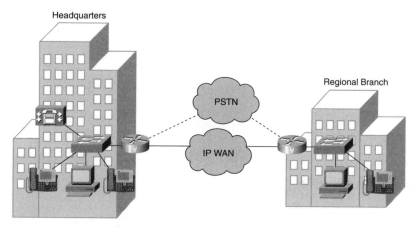

***Figure 6-3*** *The Enterprise Convergence Environment*

Figure 6-3 shows the elimination of the PBX. More specifically, however, it demonstrates the elimination of costly, duplicate equipment for voice communications at each location.

Convergence helps with ROI because it leverages the company's other investments. For example, the purchase of data equipment would already be budgeted by companies moving into a new building. The data switch that is purchased can also terminate the phones as well, if they are IP devices. So this eliminates the need to purchase voice ports (line cards). The IP port now handles both voice and data, without loss of function. For reliability and availability concerns, redundancy can be built into this design, just as it is in the traditional TDM PBX environment.

This concept is shown clearly in Figure 6-4. The data switch is capable of supporting both the data workstation as well as the voice IP phone. So, in this case, purchasing a single device (data switch) handles both the voice and data connectivity requirements. A separate chassis (i.e., PBX cabinet) is not necessary.

***Figure 6-4*** *A Single Interface for Voice and Data*

However, the real architectural savings come as a result of what is depicted in Figure 6-5. Here, the IP nature of the voice terminal (IP phone) is fully realized through the use of the integrated data switch inside the phone. Instead of connecting the data workstation (laptop or PC) to the data switch in the closet or the core, this workstation connects to the switch inside the phone. The benefit of this is that the number of ports required to support a user's voice and data needs is reduced by half. Furthermore, it also reduces the cable plant in half, as multiple cable drops to the desktop are no longer required.

***Figure 6-5*** *A Single, Shared Port for Voice and Data*

In a real-world example, a company location with 500 employees, 400 of which have laptop or desktop PCs, can realize significant savings. In a pre-convergence environment, the company must purchase and deploy 800 ports to support its voice and data requirements—one port each for voice and data. IP telephony allows the company to cut that number in half, purchasing and deploying only one port per user.

From a trunking perspective, IPT introduces favorable conditions as well. Figure 6-6 shows the traditional trunking facilities that previously were terminated in a separate PBX chassis now terminated within a router at that company location.

Headquarters

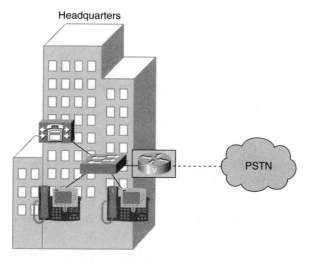

**Figure 6-6** *Terminating Voice Trunks on the IP Network*

In Figure 6-6, the trunks that previously were housed inside the PBX cabinet are now terminated on the IP network. This can be accomplished either by inserting a trunk card into the router, as shown, or into selected data switches. Therefore, because the investment is going to be made into the router and switch anyway, adding public switched telephone network (PSTN) connectivity is as easy as adding a card to either of these devices, as opposed to inserting an entirely new cabinet into the network—although that also is an option where there are concerns over existing levels of utilization for the network devices.

From a financial perspective, this now means that both line cards and trunk cards are integrated into network components, which eliminates the need for duplicate equipment for voice and data.

Finally, the call set-up and tear-down functions performed by the PBX are now performed by a web-based server application. The key here is that this is a network application. Network applications can be reached or accessed by network clients anywhere in the network. So, wherever the corporate network has been extended, voice devices anywhere in the network can access the call server application.

---

**NOTE**  Convergence takes a single call control platform in a centralized location and logically extends it wherever the network touches—a more cost-effective model than putting a PBX box in every single location.

---

Imagine a company with locations in seven cities: Los Angeles, Dallas, Chicago, Atlanta, New York City, Toronto, and London. In a Cisco Systems environment, the call control server application is called Cisco CallManager. CallManager can be shared across multiple servers in a cluster for redundancy and availability.

So, as Figure 6-7 shows, a single CallManager cluster colocated in Chicago and Dallas becomes the call control server for this entire network. The servers in Chicago and Dallas act as one system; they are managed as one system and, therefore, are in fact, a single system. Any phone or voice client on this network gets its service from the CallManager server located in Chicago.

Consider what this means:

- CallManager servers are purchased and deployed in Dallas and Chicago.

- No CallManager servers are purchased for Los Angeles, Toronto, New York City, Atlanta, or London (a valuable cost and administration savings).

- Trunk cards for each city to access the PSTN are located within existing switches or routers at those cities where phones are located.

- Line cards for phones in these cities where phones are located are the same ports that previously terminated only data.

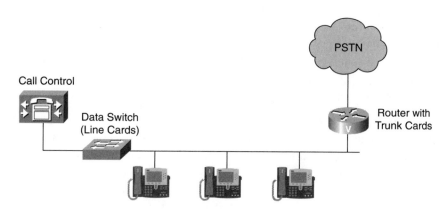

**Figure 6-7** *The Network Is the PBX*

In this example, the company has saved itself the purchase of five PBXs with duplicate line and trunk connectivity. Cabling is simplified so that a single drop to the desktop handles both voice and data users. Also, because purchasing data switches and routers was a requirement anyway, the only additional purchase required, if the network is designed properly, are CallManager servers for Dallas and Chicago, trunk cards for each location, and phones. The price of the PBX cabinet, TDM environment, line cards, trunk cards, and CPUs are eliminated for five different locations.

# Administration Costs

The ability to reduce the overhead of MAC is just one factor in ROI. Users take care of more things for themselves, thus saving time, money, and resources administratively.

A single cable plant means not wondering which jack to plug into (and therefore, not placing a call to a help desk or administration). It allows users to move their phones to a conference room for the afternoon, or even enter an ID into the phone already there, and not bothering the IS/telecom staff. It also allows users in a wireless environment to take their laptops from meeting to meeting throughout the building, with their phone calls following them on their laptop.

Taken separately, these types of benefits can be trivialized. Yet taken in their entirety, they create an environment of empowered employees and streamlined support staffs, which affects the bottom line for any organization. On one hand, some people might say that reducing the dollars companies pay for MAC work is pinching pennies. However, the industry's telecommunications providers are generating hundreds of millions of dollars in MAC work annually, so *someone* is paying these companies for this service. These are budgetary dollars that are being greatly reduced by organizations moving towards convergence.

---

**NOTE**     Don't be fooled into thinking companies aren't paying much for MAC work. MAC work is the fundamental after-the-sale revenue producer for many telecommunications providers. The fact that this market has thrived for three decades is a direct result of the dollars companies spend for these services.

---

In many cases, MAC is something companies are accustomed to budgeting for—the cost of doing business. IP telephony is changing this. Not eliminating it, but changing it. After all, the databases for these new IP server-based telephony solutions don't just magically populate themselves. Someone has to enter the initial information. So technically, adds are still a reality to deal with, but moves and changes are greatly reduced. This means financial savings for many organizations that find their employees in a constant state of movement.

# Maintenance Costs

IP telephony provides a streamlined administration opportunity that can yield ongoing savings approaching or even exceeding the savings realized from the initial deployment of IPT. The savings begin with simplified administration, and the dramatic reduction of MAC. Eliminating the need to call the telecom department (or a provider service) for moves and changes to the database results in personnel savings for an organization or budgetary savings. Because much has already been discussed regarding the value of simplified administration, this section focuses mostly on the other post-install savings: maintenance.

Figure 6-8 depicts a company with four locations in a traditional voice model; that is, separate voice and data networks with PBXs installed in each location. This is the environment present in most multilocation companies today.

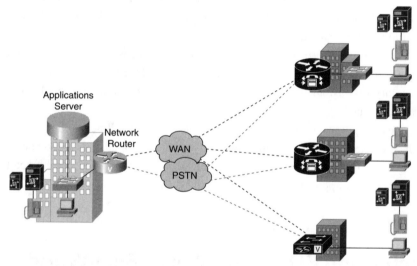

*Figure 6-8* *Maintenance in the Enterprise*

In this common scenario, the company pays maintenance fees on every piece of equipment in the network. It pays maintenance for the data switches, the routers, the application servers, and the PBXs. In a converged model, however, the maintenance on the PBX is eliminated. In its place is maintenance on the call server. This is a trade-off that most companies gladly welcome. The maintenance on the data infrastructure remains in place, but the maintenance on the telephony side is greatly reduced.

With such a compelling argument, you might wonder why IP telephony hasn't grown even more rapidly than it has. One answer is that this is a difficult proposition for those companies who manufacture PBX equipment. After all, these manufacturers, and the distributors who sell and service their technologies, heavily depend on the back-end revenues that hardware maintenance (and administration) provides. Consider that in an IPT model, this revenue now often reverts, in reduced form, to the provider of the IP network. This is an especially difficult position for manufacturers. Since 2000, market trends continue to indicate fewer companies buying traditional PBX equipment in favor of IPT solutions.

So, on one hand, the potential loss of maintenance and administration revenue is daunting. However, with the market slowly moving away from the traditional PBX in favor of IP solutions, it's almost a case of "pick your poison" for traditional PBX manufacturers.

The key for these manufacturers, as it turns out, is convincing customers (rightly so) that back-end services, albeit streamlined for the IP network, are still necessary for customers to achieve the same levels of availability to which they are accustomed.

Less equipment purchased and deployed, streamlined administration, reduced maintenance: So far, the ROI on IP telephony sounds like a good deal for companies. Even greater savings, however, occur when companies embrace the concept of new applications impacting their businesses.

# Achieving ROI: Examples of Real-World Deployments

The previous chapter touched on application development in a number of industries. The key for companies is to ensure that the potential business impact—particularly from a financial perspective—is included in the ROI calculation. The budget cost recovery often can dwarf the initial savings on equipment, or ongoing maintenance savings. Consider the following industries.

## Banking and Finance

The banking and finance industry offers the most compelling environment for IP telephony because of the numerous locations (or branches) it has in its networks, and the tremendous potential to eliminate equipment throughout those locations. Consider a small financial institution that has a main headquarters with 20 branches. Each of the 20 branches has two things: a data infrastructure interconnected with the main location, and a telephone system.

The idea of replacing 20 telephone systems with one single system that is centrally managed and supported is extremely attractive to this market. Before even considering applications, a bank that is looking to open two new branches in the coming year can realize significant savings by deploying IP telephony today. A bank that has deployed CallManager servers at the main location, for example, need only deploy trunk cards and phones at the new branches. It does not need a new phone system. It can use the data switches required for data connectivity to terminate phones, and simply install a T1 or PRI trunk card into the router. Deploying voice to the new branches is as easy as installing one card and sending out phones in boxes. The necessary database work to set up the new users is handled centrally, at the main headquarters.

At the beginning of this chapter, I described how Cisco opened its Richardson campus in Texas. Users simply opened the box containing their new phone and plugged it in. The same environment is available to banks today. Banks and secondary schools are primary beneficiaries of this new environment because of the number of locations they have to support.

## K–12 Education

Secondary education, or grades Kindergarten through 12, is one of the fastest growing sectors in the IP telephony market. Consider a suburban school district with a total of 30 schools spread between elementary, junior high, and high schools. The school district likely has an administration building as well.

IP telephony allows the school district to install the system at the administration building, and use the IP network to reach all the schools in the district. A single cluster handling call set-up and release at the administration location saves the district the cost of purchasing and deploying 30 different telephone systems.

Take this solution out of the suburbs and into the city. Now the school district doesn't have just 30 schools, but potentially hundreds. The same model applies. The budget need only cover a single cluster (even if it is spread across two locations) of servers eliminating the need to purchase hundreds of different telephone systems. The savings potential is staggering, just from an initial procurement perspective.

This is the initial ROI factor driving companies towards IP telephony. Even if a company has only one location, when it is time to replace the existing phone system, converging onto the IP network is financially compelling. However, after deployment in this environment, then the ongoing potential savings must also be accounted for in an ROI discussion.

## Retail Organizations

Large retail organizations spend significant amounts of money on their internal help desks. Most large retail institutions, whether they are grocery stores or department stores, use point-of-sale (POS) equipment that is tied into their corporate data network. Yet, when they have problems with the equipment or need to call the company help desk for any reason, that call is usually placed across toll-free lines.

As with any call center or automatic call distribution (ACD) environment, the number of agents/support reps/help personnel who answer the phones is normally less than the number of callers at any one time. So, calls get queued in line, waiting for an agent to become available to take their call. Even though the store personnel calling into the help desk are calling on a toll-free number, the company is still paying for usage of those trunks associated with the toll-free number.

A discussion I had with one organization revealed average wait times of three to four minutes for their help desk. Now, if these are four- or five-digit calls being handled locally, that is one thing, but when these are calls placed to a toll-free number, then the costs associated with such an event increase significantly.

In this example, the retail company has over 2000 stores across the United States. Let's make the following assumptions:

- On any given day, half of those stores make a minimum of one call into the help desk/service center, therefore, approximately 1000 calls.

- The average wait time is 4 minutes, with an average cost of .05 cents per minute on the toll-free trunks.

- The average duration of a call is 10 minutes.

With these assumptions, you can estimate that 1000 calls × 4 minutes × $0.05 per call equals $200 per day as the cost of callers waiting in queue. Also, 1000 calls × 10 minutes × $0.05 per call, equals $500 per day as the cost of any one call, including hold time and talk time. Assuming a 6-day workweek, the following applies:

- The weekly costs for wait time is $200 × 6 days, or $1200.

- The weekly costs for any one call, including hold time and talk time, are $500 × 6 days, or $3000.

Extrapolating this over 52 weeks, it is estimated that 1000 calls per day will cost the company $156,000 in total calls, including hold time and talk time. However, of that $156,000, roughly $62,400 is the cost of hold/queue time for callers.

It is this latter number, the $62,400, that can be dramatically addressed by IP telephony applications.

The potential application in question takes advantage of the fact that the device placing the call (the IP phone in the store) is an IP device. Because this is an IP client, the application knows (or can know) two important things about the phone: its IP address, as an IP client for integrated data sessions; and its extension number for voice sessions (i.e., phone calls).

This is critical, because this organization can develop a new process and a new application that allows the store personnel to simply press a button on the phone that launches a data session with the application, thereby avoiding calls to a toll-free number.

This new application, sitting in the call center/help desk, is monitoring the status of the center. The application tracks how many calls have come in that day, and can provide the average number of calls for the past 30 days. It can show historical trends, calculate the average wait time, and identify how many people are waiting in queue at any given moment. It also tracks how many help desk personnel are logged in at the moment, and therefore, who is available to help.

So when Sarah, who is a manager for one of the Dallas-based stores, places a call into the help desk, she is actually pressing a button or icon on her phone that launches an application. This application, as an IP client, interacts with the application located at the support center. The two applications determine that Sarah is going to be the tenth caller in queue, and can expect to wait seven minutes to be answered by a live help desk representative. The application can display this information to Sarah on the screen of her IP phone.

Most importantly, however, the central application places Sarah in queue, using her IP address as the placeholder. Notice now, Sarah has not made a phone call. She is not using trunk resources while waiting in queue. She has initiated a data session that is using the bandwidth on the company IP network, extended across the enterprise. So Sarah is in queue, but the company is not incurring a per-minute charge for this wait time.

Further, the application knows that Sarah has an IP phone with a display screen. So the application audibly tells Sarah how many people are ahead of her in the queue and the expected hold time, and it provides this information to her visually, on her phone. Finally, the application periodically updates the current status. Depending upon the thresholds set, the application could update visually every 30 seconds, every 60 seconds, etc.

In this example, the application is programmed to continually monitor the status of each user in queue. Sarah can save a significant amount of time and company money by not waiting in queue on company voice trunks. For example, Sarah might have been number 22 in queue when she initially pressed her icon to call the support center. Any amount of time could have passed while 17 users were handled until only 4 were ahead of her. That amount of time is now saved, both in Sarah's productivity and company finances.

Now, consider this: The productivity savings occur because Sarah is *not on the phone waiting to be connected*. She knows that 21 people are in front of her, so Sarah can continue working, *including placing new phone calls*. The application continues to monitor the status, giving her frequent updates *visually* on her phone, letting her know how many people are still ahead of her. Now Sarah can end her current call, stop whatever she might have been doing, and prepare for the incoming call from the help desk.

A company can use many parameters to queue, prioritize, or identify requests. For example, a caller's IP address can be used as a placeholder until only four people are in queue ahead of them, *or* three minutes of wait time have elapsed— whichever condition occurs first.

The key, of course, is to drive down the connect time for callers waiting to be handled. As described earlier, these savings alone can be fairly significant. The final consideration, however, might be not as obvious.

Consider that the number of trunks required at the help desk location are sized based on the number of callers expected to be handled by the help desk personnel and the maximum number of callers that will be supported in queue. Because the objective of this application is to drive down costs by limiting the number of people who are holding in queue using trunk facilities, this means the incoming trunk groups can be sized with fewer trunks.

Therefore, the company saves money not only in terms of trunk usage (in minutes), but also in the number of trunks required. Eliminating trunks can mean eliminating a fixed monthly expense. Reducing the connect time for callers in queue means eliminating a variable daily expense. This type of IP telephony application can dramatically affect both of these types of expenses.

## *It Seemed Like a Good Idea at the Time...*

This example is important because most companies spend a great deal of time trying to control expenses in their call center environments that deal with external callers, such as customers, partners, or suppliers. However, most of the conversations I've had with companies regarding their internal support desks have a different tone. Often, they are smaller, of course. However, with large, multilocation retail firms, they can be quite large, and their approach often becomes a double-edged sword.

One company I recall downsized their internal support center, reducing the number of people by "a few" as it indicated. One person that was affected actually was redeployed into a different role. So, his salary and benefits were still on the company payroll. Still, the support center was downsized.

Subsequently, however, this meant fewer people to answer calls. This is not a problem if the number of calls and callers reduces appropriately as well. However, this was not the case. So now, it had fewer support people answering the same number of calls. In order to support this, the company ultimately had to increase the number of trunks (as users were not accustomed to holding so long or getting busy signals).

*continues*

> ### *It Seemed Like a Good Idea at the Time... (Continued)*
>
> So, the company saved money in personnel, but saw the monthly trunk costs increase, as well as the monthly trunk usage. These new costs didn't immediately match the savings provided by eliminating a few salaries, but over time, it would have approached this point.
>
> The irony, as told to me, was that over time, the company ended up placing resources back into the support center—but neglected to subsequently reduce the number of trunks! So, months later, this company ended up with the same number of support personnel, the same number of calls—and more trunks.

# ROI Conclusions

In summary, the opportunities for cost savings are found in three areas:

- **Network costs**—Savings are usually seen in the procurement of equipment. For new buildings, data equipment—such as switches and routers—is a given. If the network can be designed so that these components also support the connectivity and communications for voice, then companies have just significantly reduced the capital outlay required.

- **Administration costs**—Savings are typically seen with the reduction in MAC, as well as the reduction in maintenance costs on an annual basis. This is a true opportunity for cost recovery, recapturing potential dollars budgeted each year and considered the cost of doing business.

- **Application impact**—Savings can be realized through new applications that improve business processes, resulting in potential revenue gain, and often resulting in cost reductions in areas that have nothing to do with telecommunications.

Finally, in a convergence model, calculating ROI for convergence is an exercise that asks companies to step outside their comfort zones and confront scenarios, practices, and processes that might be uncomfortable or even embarrassing. This openness is particularly critical when investigating new applications that will alter or enhance business processes, because the application might need to be developed to target the company's needs.

Many of these applications do not exist today. This is important to remember. They are laying dormant in an organization, waiting for someone to bring them to light. Because these applications are written to interface with existing back-end systems, using industry-standard interfaces, protocols, and languages, these applications can be developed much more quickly (and less expensively) than people realize.

In addition, the potential impact of these applications is limited only by how open-minded organizations are. The biggest killer for these potential applications is the notion that, "This is how we've always done things." This approach is essentially saying, "This is how we do business. It's how we've always done business. The costs that are associated with this are built into our budget. We don't worry about how we can reduce these costs!"

Defeating these paradigms is key to winning the ROI battle in terms of applications. Most manufacturers who provide IP telephony solutions also provide tools to help with ROI calculations. These tools require companies to open up their books (and minds) and share them with their partners, who can help them identify potential areas of business impact, as well as traditional telecommunications savings. Selecting the right partner, therefore, is of utmost importance, not only for the realization of ROI, but for the overall viability of the solution selected. This is the topic for the next chapter.

# CHAPTER 7

# WATCH THAT FIRST STEP

In December 2001, while still at Cisco Systems, I had the opportunity to host the Cisco IP Telephony Users Group. Some people still believe this industry is in early adoption mode. However, the fact that Cisco has hundreds of customers who now make up their Users Group is a strong indication that customers have moved beyond the "kick the tires" phase.

I bring this Users Group meeting into discussion because one of the key things we learned at Cisco from this meeting was the fact that many customers were having problems directly associated with their selection of a deployment partner.

"We've had a lot of problems, but found that the system worked fine after we got rid of _____."

Fill in the blank with the names of various partners and providers, and you have an accurate description of how a number of customers felt. Many customers experienced problems with their deployments that had little to do with the product or technology, but had everything to do with the design and deployment practices of the partner they had selected.

Three critical questions face a company when it looks to deploy IP telephony. The first two are fairly obvious.

The first question is: Why make this investment? In other words, why adopt IP telephony? What benefits will an organization gain from this convergence deployment?

The second question is: What is the return on this investment? What is the economic payback a company can expect?

The first two questions have been discussed in previous chapters. The final question is one that is sometimes overlooked: Who do I select to partner with me on this journey?

This question is often as important, if not more important, than the choice of manufacturer. In far too many instances, IPT works flawlessly in a company where thousands of IP phones are deployed—yet across the city, a company with 150 phones is having huge difficulties getting the product to work.

It's the same product in both cases. So what is different? Can selecting the right partner solve this problem?

This chapter focuses on identifying those steps that are critical to the successful deployment of IP telephony, including steps to get the network ready, and creating a comprehensive plan that accounts for potential obstacles, many of which can be predicted.

# Understanding the Impact of Voice Traffic

It all begins with the network. Some networks are ready for voice deployments. Most are not. Exactly what must be done to get a network ready for voice is the question at hand. The answer to this question varies from company to company. Every network is different, and the load placed on every network is different. So, although standard white papers might help one understand potential areas of impact, they are not going to solve this problem. Each customer has unique cultural, technical, and organizational issues that must be considered during the planning stages.

Remember that IP telephony is all about taking voice away from an isolated, protected environment and placing it on the network. This is not to say that the network is not safe. It simply means that in a PBX environment, whenever a user picked up the phone, he or she was guaranteed to have a 64 K slice of bandwidth. The user was also guaranteed that whatever else was going on inside the data/IP network had no impact *whatsoever* on voice communications sessions.

In other words, no matter if large downloads were in progress, batch transmissions of financial data, video-on-demand sessions in progress, or just hundreds (or thousands) of network saves and updates in the works—none of these occurrences had any impact on voice at all.

In an IP telephony environment, this assurance changes. That is not to say that it won't work on your network. It simply means that certain tasks must be performed to determine what impact, if any, data sessions are going to have on your voice sessions. Furthermore, you must determine what impact, if any, voice is going to have on your data network and its applications. To do this, companies must make sure that the partner they select has the competency and experience to make these evaluations.

Therefore, in an IP telephony deployment, various tasks that had no impact on the PBX can now potentially impact voice communications that originate on and transverse the IP network. These tasks include the following:

- Saving and retrieving files to/from a network-mapped drive
- Accessing, sending, and retrieving e-mails
- Downloading or run-time streaming of video content from web pages (internal or external)

- Downloading files from web pages
- Downloading music/videos from search engines
- Instant messaging
- Any access to internal or external web pages

Every one of these activities, which likely happens on a regular basis any day of the week in the workplace, can have an impact on voice communications that now run on the network via IP telephony. Each of these activities, in a PBX environment, had absolutely *no* impact at all on voice communications.

So, the question is, how much (if any) impact will these activities have on voice? Furthermore, how much impact will placing all the voice communications on the network have on these activities?

The right partner is going to have a good blend of experience with both voice and data communications. On one hand, these are voice applications and voice technologies, so you need someone who understands traditional voice, PBXs, voice messaging, contact centers, etc. At the same time, these applications and technologies are now running on a different network—the data network. So, an understanding of data technologies (such as switches, routers, servers, and associated protocols, applications, and management techniques) is critical as well. The issue that many customers have faced during their initial deployments has been driven by the fact that they have engaged a partner who has *one* of the necessary skill sets, but not both.

As companies are finding, they face a number of challenges when deploying IP telephony. As noted, many of these challenges center around the IP network. The good news is that most of these network challenges are predictable. Many of the potential problems that an organization might encounter can be anticipated, and action plans can be developed to address them *prior* to the actual deployment. However, most organizations do not do this.

Without a doubt, the biggest challenge faced by my current team in Professional Services is convincing customers to do their homework up front and to conduct the necessary due diligence required to ensure a successful deployment. Admittedly, this challenge is getting easier with each story of IPT deployments gone awry, but the fact remains that customers too often cause themselves unnecessary pains and risks by not assessing their current network environment.

## The Data Environment

Toni Baych, president and principal consultant for Vertex Consulting, was one of the earliest consultants I had the opportunity to work with in the convergence market. Vertex has a particular competency with health care organizations, and a great understanding of the potential impact of IP telephony for these companies. At a recent lunch, I asked her to share with me her list of top priorities companies should have when undertaking a convergence project. Number one on her list was to "assess network infrastructure to determine existing viability and/or modifications required including associate costs."

Step one is to assess the current state of the IP network. Remember, the IP network in place in most organizations as of 2003 is, for the most part, a network that was designed to handle the transmission and exchange of data, and possibly video. Said a different way, these networks were *not* designed to handle voice sessions—and voice sessions are different from data, in virtually every way:

- Data sessions are often transaction-oriented. Voice sessions are not.

- Data sessions occur in bursts. Voice sessions can last for hours (conference calls, for example).

- Data will put an occasional stress load on the network, whereas voice will put a constant load on the network.

- Data sessions can recover well from delays caused by the network. Voice sessions recover far less efficiently, and are far more noticeable to the user. Furthermore, data sessions typically aren't as sensitive to latency as voice sessions.

Most companies have a network in place that has been designed and built for one type of traffic, and now the company plans to place voice traffic onto the network—a type of traffic that behaves differently, reacts to network pressures differently, and performs differently. Getting the existing IP network ready to take on this new challenge is the first step in any deployment activity.

The concept of a network assessment certainly is not limited to IP telephony. It might be argued that it is a good practice to conduct these assessments periodically as new users and new applications are added. Although this sounds like a decent idea for most IP applications, it is absolutely critical when adding voice to the mix.

A typical network assessment is going to verify utilization and software levels of key components on the network, such as core and edge switches, and edge routers. Utilization levels are important because, depending on the manufacturer, IP telephony might place an additional load on the component.

For example, in a Cisco environment, PSTN connectivity is achieved through the installation of a trunk card (referred to as a blade or module) into a switch or router. This is a cost-efficient and easily achievable means of connecting the IP network to the public telephone network. However, it means that an additional load is going to be placed on this device, so assessing the device's current utilization is required prior to adding any additional load to it. Also, it is necessary to verify that the router chassis in question can accommodate that type of blade, and whether the current IOS will even support the required features.

In other manufacturers' environments, this might not be the case. Many PBX manufacturers, for example, do not use the IP components to terminate PSTN equipment. Instead of placing a trunk card inside a switch or a router, they place these cards in a separate chassis or cabinet that they provide. This practice has benefits and drawbacks. The benefit is that you don't have to worry about switch or router utilization because the new chassis will absorb the added utilization. However, the drawback is that by adding another chassis or cabinet into the network, you have just added additional costs—both procurement and for ongoing maintenance—and this can adversely impact efforts for a rapid ROI. This approach also assumes that physical space exists in the company to house additional cabinets.

As the market leader, however, Cisco finds that many customers embrace the concept of fully using network resources to accommodate IP telephony. So, assessing the current state of these components is critical to the success of the overall project.

In my current capacity, my team is responsible for helping customers get their networks in shape to handle voice calls without impact on availability or quality. Voice readiness assessments are a staple of our internal process. As we tell customers constantly, assessing their network is something we have to do anyway. The choice is *when* will we perform this task?

We can perform this assessment up front, in a comfortable setting, prior to the deployment, for a fixed and aggressively priced cost to the customer. Or, we can wait until called in after a hundred or more phones have been deployed, and the solution isn't working, calls are being dropped, quality is poor, someone's credibility (if not his job) is on the line, and emotions are running high. The customer ends up paying an hourly rate at this point, and spends far more than he would have for an assessment up front.

In most cases, we end up performing this service anyway. So it is to the customer's benefit to have it done up front, and then use what is learned from the assessment to select the technology, design the solution, and deploy it easily and cost-effectively.

A good analogy is a puzzle stored in a plain white cardboard box. Inside the box are 1000 puzzle pieces, but you don't know what the ultimate picture is supposed to look like. Your challenge is to put all the pieces together.

Can you do it? Certainly, but it's going to take you some time. You're going to make a lot of mistakes. Some pieces that look like they should go together actually aren't even related. Yet, you don't know this because you don't know what the picture is supposed to look like. It could be a nature scene, a cityscape, or a portrait. You'll find this out through individually assessing (there's that word) every piece. You might separate the outer edge pieces, and try to work your way in.

The analogy is eerily similar to how many companies are trying to deploy IP telephony. They have multiple sites. They don't know what the ultimate solution is going to look like. They don't have a good understanding of the pieces they have in place and how they are performing, but there they go, starting on the outer edges, deploying IPT on the edges of their network, and working their way in.

This is the worst way to deploy IP telephony simply because in this case, we don't know what we don't know! We might run into problems that were totally unexpected, and initially, we are at a loss as to how to resolve them. At this point, we begin doing what we should have done in the first place—assess the network, find out where and why we have points of latency, high utilization, lack of bandwidth, no process for administering quality of service.

The alternative to assessing these components is one of the following: Buy all new components, or take your chances.

Some companies have literally torn out their entire infrastructure to prepare for IP telephony without determining if it is necessary. Although this makes the manufacturer and its associated distribution partners happy, it certainly has an adverse affect on ROI.

This is not to say that a new data infrastructure might not be necessary—the point is that an assessment is the first step to discover how much of a new infrastructure is required.

Buying a brand-new infrastructure unnecessarily might sound far-fetched. However, the vast majority of customers actually just "roll the dice" and deploy hundreds of IP phones on their existing networks without making any changes to the network and without performing any due diligence to see what impact these new users are going to have on the network.

The goal is to maintain the same level of service, availability, and voice clarity, *each and every time* the user picks up the telephone for the entire duration of the call, no matter what else is occurring on the network. So, assessing current utilization levels is a key component of the network assessment process. Again, the real question is this: What impact will all the existing data applications have on voice communications? The safest way to answer this question is to conduct what is referred to as a *voice readiness assessment (VRA)*.

# VRA

The purpose of a VRA is to determine precisely what impact the data network is going to have on voice. When we place voice on the existing IP network, what is going to happen? In other words, this is just proper planning—taking into account all the information we have at our disposal, and using it correctly. It starts with having the right information available in the first place.

The easiest and safest way to understand the impact of convergence is to test it. Put a sampling of voice sessions on the IP network and step back to see what happens. The industry has tools available to help with this process. NetIQ, for example, provides a platform to help assess the impact of voice on the network, and vice versa.

Many customers who deploy voice experience problems such as one-way audio, dropped calls, and static/clipped calls. Tools are available to help identify where (and why) these conditions might exist. Placing voice on the network, in a simulated environment, is a safe way to stress the network. The goal is to see if the network starts to degrade—and to see how well voice will be handled by the network—but it doesn't stop here.

It's one thing to place 10–15 voice sessions on the network and assess the impact. However, to fully understand how adding voice will impact the data network, you must understand the current traffic loads. The real question a company must answer is this: How is *your* existing voice traffic going to impact *your* existing IP network? This is the question that a white paper or a research report from an analyst is not going to adequately address. Both of these documents are important to help educate companies about this emerging environment, but neither identifies what happens to your own network when you deploy IPT.

This is where the competency of your partners comes into play. A partner who knows how to assess your current voice environment, assess your network, and use that knowledge to determine the impact of your voice on your network is a valuable asset in the convergence journey.

So, a true VRA doesn't start with the network, but with the original PBX. A voice traffic study can determine call volumes, durations, etc. What businesses need to do, therefore, is conduct a PBX traffic study to determine the existing voice requirements of the company, then take that information and superimpose it on top of the IP network.

In other words, if the traffic study shows that a company has an average 200 voice sessions going on at any one time, and the average duration for these sessions (i.e., phone calls) is 3 minutes, then that is the environment that, at a minimum, should be tested on the network.

If the traffic study shows that every Monday morning at 9 A.M., 35 people take part in a conference call that lasts generally 1 hour, then that scenario should also be tested on the network.

---

**NOTE**    The VRA is an attempt to get a realistic look at what should happen when a company's voice traffic is deployed across their IP network.

---

The purpose of a VRA is to identify the peak periods, the average number of calls, and the call durations, and then use this data to determine the call load that will stress the network. A true VRA, therefore, gives a good prediction of how well a company's IP network will accommodate that company's typical voice traffic.

The result of such a stress test shows a company exactly where any problems are likely to occur by deploying voice onto their IP network, as is. Latency spots, configuration or design issues that might impact voice, faulty codecs—these types of scenarios come to light by stressing the network with real-voice parameters.

# Timing Is Everything: Identify Problems Before They Occur

Most company IP networks were not designed for voice. They weren't built to accommodate hundreds or thousands of voice sessions each day. They were designed for a more data-centric purpose. It is common sense to assess how well the network will react to these new users and their sessions.

However, recall the fact that convergence is all about change. This is one of those instances. The idea of paying for an assessment of the current environment (or current state) as preparation for deploying a new telephone system is a radical change for most companies. As discussed, IP telephony is far more than just a new telephone system. However, as most people within a company's procurement process do not realize this just yet, they resist spending money on a function that they believe has been free in the past.

The reality is that this prework in the traditional PBX environment was not free, but was built into the price of the installation. In an IP environment, this cost is more significant, and more difficult to hide within the scope of the installation.

Therefore, many organizations resist this necessary step. Unfortunately, all too often, they pay for this decision in dramatic ways. Problems associated with deploying IP telephony have little to do with the actual voice communications platform, and everything to do with the condition and design of the network itself. The still-short history of IPT is inundated with examples of network issues causing problems for voice communications.

The key point is that when these problems occur, the company installing IPT is likely to come to the conclusion that this new system does not work. This is an incorrect assumption—the system works fine, but the network needs some fine-tuning, if not a complete overhaul.

Let me share the experiences of a number of clients who decided to deploy IP telephony without first conducting a full network assessment. In these cases, network issues, such as a lack of bandwidth and poor resource utilization, undermined the success of the IPT deployment. The following sections review some of these challenges and discuss various potential actions that can address these concerns.

## Lack of WAN Bandwidth

Probably the most memorable installation that went awry because of bandwidth issues occurred very early in the evolution of IP telephony. In 1999, a company installed IP phones between two locations, as shown in Figure 7-1.

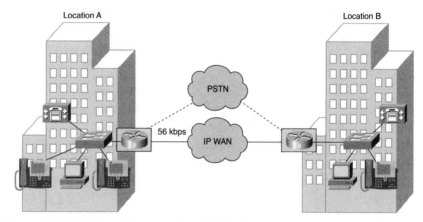

***Figure 7-1*** *WAN Considerations for IP Telephony*

A couple of points are key in this diagram. First of all, this installation occurred before Cisco CallManager control servers could be centralized to support an entire enterprise network. So CallManager servers are at both locations to handle call control. The second point is this installation occurred during the early days of compression, and this company was not using any compression on the WAN.

There were about 30 users at Location A and another 70 or so users at Location B. The company WAN supported 56 K transmissions between the two locations. So, the question one might ask is, "How could people make calls between locations?" The answer was simple: They couldn't.

A single call, uncompressed, on the WAN would use 64 K of bandwidth plus overhead. This came out to approximately 80 K of bandwidth. Because of insufficient bandwidth on the WAN to accommodate calls between locations across the company network, the company had to continue paying for long-distance calls between these two locations until they added capacity to their WAN.

A logical question to be asked is why didn't they add capacity *before* the installation? That is not an easy question to answer, but it was clear that this customer had bought into the concept that IP telephony was going to save them a lot of money.

As previously discussed, IP telephony is most likely going to result in cost savings across many functions—but it is going to require an investment, and therefore, in many cases, the cost savings will occur over a period of time—hence an ROI calculation is in order. This customer, however, wasn't prepared to make that investment up front. After all, everything he had read in trade publications and technical write-ups talked about the tremendous (and immediate) savings associated with IPT. So the idea of adding bandwidth (and costs) to the network was not an acceptable decision at that time.

As a result, this company ended up with a system that made local, internal calls wonderfully, but still needed to pass calls between the two locations out through the PSTN.

A simple WAN analysis would have shown this customer that its current WAN could not support voice calls. Remember: In a converged environment, the company WAN has to carry both voice and data calls, and do so *simultaneously*.

## Router Utilization

Another customer had a multilocation network in place. The data infrastructure was Cisco-based, but the IP telephony solution installed was from a PBX manufacturer. The problems that this customer encountered were, for the most part, because of the network. One key problem was due in part to software from the PBX manufacturer, but the overall situation was a perfect example of the necessity of a VRA.

Figure 7-2 shows the layout for this organization. A key point is that this company designed this network so that the majority of calls coming in for the branch locations actually came in to the main location first, and were then directed to the branch locations.

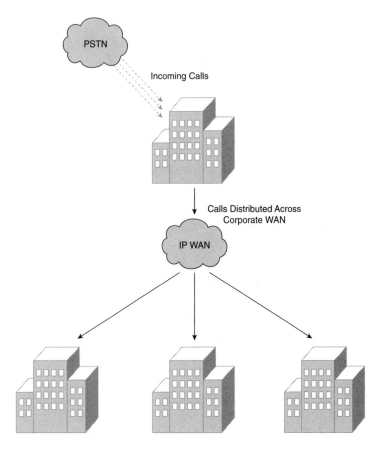

*Figure 7-2* *Calls Distributed Across Corporate WAN*

First, it's important to note that no readiness assessment was conducted on the network prior to this installation. Like many other companies, this company decided to roll the dice and take its chances that its network was suitable for voice

(133)

without any modifications. The results of this decision were the following problems:

- Callers experienced constant one-way audio.
- Callers were losing connections (dropped calls).
- Callers experienced excessive echo during calls.
- Voice mail quality was poor.

## One-Way Audio

This customer's one-way audio problem was fairly easy to reproduce and diagnose. The core router at the main location was experiencing very high CPU utilization. This router's high CPU utilization was creating a memory buffer problem that resulted in voice packets being dropped. These dropped packets caused the one-way audio situation. Remember, most calls were coming into this main location and then being distributed across the company WAN to the branches. So, although there was plenty of WAN capacity, the router was running on empty and, therefore, couldn't process the calls.

The first step in reducing the high CPU utilization was to turn off unneeded features. On all routers, Cisco Discovery Protocol (CDP) was disabled. This feature was unnecessary because the IP endpoints were not Cisco IP phones, nor did they support the CDP.

The next step was to replace the customer's Cisco 1605 router with a Cisco 3640 router loaned to the customer for troubleshooting. After installing the 3640, the problem of one-way calls was eliminated. Subsequently, the customer purchased a new 3640 router. Previously, the Cisco 1605 router was at times running at 90 percent utilization. However, the data applications on the network recovered from the delays caused by dropped packets and retransmitted packets because of this overutilization. Voice applications, however, being more time-sensitive, could not recover from those same delays. Hence, calls would experience one-way symptoms. After installing the 3640, utilization never exceeded 40 percent.

## Losing Connected Calls

The second major problem reported by the customer was calls being disconnected and dropped entirely. It was discovered that the quality of service (QoS) configuration in the routers had been changed so that call set-up and control packets were not being placed in the priority queue. In an IP telephony session with this PBX manufacturer, these control packets are necessary to maintain existing voice calls. Without the call control packets in priority queues, there were times when the IPT system would drop voice connections, thus causing calls to be dropped.

Additionally, the high CPU utilization of the core router, as previously discussed, also came into play with this problem. To address this issue of QoS configurations in the router, the access lists in routers were updated to correctly process control packets. IP-PBXs were then able to keep voice communication constantly active after these changes were implemented, thus preserving QoS and preventing calls from being dropped.

## Excessive Echo During Calls

The excessive echo turned out to be the easiest problem to solve. In two instances, users complained of an echo in their calls. In the first instance, the source of the echo was determined to be introduced by a headset. The second was found to be a defective phone. Replacing these two devices solved this problem, which would have been diagnosed during a VRA. Instead, troubleshooting time that cost this customer additional money for services could have been saved, and a deployment could have gone more smoothly.

## Voice Mail Quality

The voice mail problem was the most difficult to troubleshoot and resolve. Figure 7-3 depicts the call flow experienced by users, and the ultimate cause of the voice quality problems with their voice-mail system.

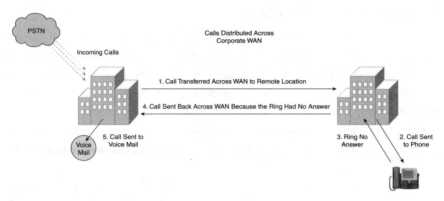

***Figure 7-3*** *WAN Directed Call Flow*

As shown in Figure 7-3, a call would be placed to the main location with the intended party located at Branch B. The call was transmitted across the corporate WAN to Branch B, where it would be handled by the IP-PBX at this location. After ringing four times without an answer (a "ring no answer" condition), the call would be transferred back across the corporate WAN to the main location and then sent to the corporate voice-mail system.

Upon recreating the scenario, we discovered that while processing calls into the voice-mail system, the IP-PBX system was performing a function commonly referred to as *tromboning*. When a call comes in from the PSTN, and the core IP-PBX determines that the call needs to be sent to a remote site, it opens a voice channel to the remote IP-PBX.

The remote system then sent the call to the appropriate phone. If the employee did not answer the call after a set number of rings (in this case, four rings), the remote IP-PBX opened a *second* voice channel back to the core in the main location for forwarding to the voice-mail system.

This meant that a call into the main location was converted from TDM to G.723 encoding at the core for LAN handling and transmission on the WAN.

The call was then converted from G.723 back to TDM at the remote site. When there was a ring no answer condition, that call was converted *back* from TDM to G.723 for forwarding to the core PBX.

Then, the core IP-PBX converted the G.723 call back to an analog signal to be sent to the voice-mail system, resulting in poor voice quality. This is the equivalent of taking a printed document, making a reduced copy of it, then taking the smaller document, putting it on another copier, and enlarging it again. Imagine repeating this entire process: The result is a document that is not as clear as the original. The cause was not as straightforward as the other problems that have been discussed. The reason that voice-mail audio quality was so poor at times was because of the architecture of the selected IP-PBX system. This particular system, at that time, did not have an effective algorithm to deal with the tromboning effect. Enhancements have since been made to this platform to correct this. However, the issue the customer faced could have been predicted with an up-front assessment and proper design considerations.

In the interim, we ended up changing the codec setting in the IP-PBX from G.723 to G.711 for one of the remote sites to improve the quality of the voice-mail messages. The G.711 codec has a much higher sampling rate and, as such, the quality of the signal presented to the voice-mail system was improved. The downside to this, of course, is that the G.711 codec uses more of the available bandwidth and therefore was not a permanent solution to the problem.

It's important to note that the initial reaction of this customer (as it is with most customers I have had the privilege of working with) was to point the finger at the IP-PBX. If voice calls were being dropped, if audio was bad or one-way, obviously, there must be something wrong with the system itself. In reality, only the final problem discussed (the tromboning issue with calls transferred into voice mail) was the result of the telephone system itself.

The point is this: Without conducting an assessment up front, problem resolution is like stumbling around in the dark. You have no baseline, no objective starting point, no understanding of the network that is documented. So all this information has to be learned at the outset.

## Response Time

The last example is of a Norstan customer who took the preferred approach and had a VRA prior to deploying IP telephony. Even in this case, it took a bit of convincing to get this customer to conduct this assessment. Like most companies, he was convinced his network was fine. The reason for the confidence was not unfounded.

As far as the company was concerned, it wasn't experiencing any significant network problems. In other words, its users weren't complaining about response times, so everything must be fine. However, up to this point, this company was only running data applications on its network, and data applications are extremely resilient. These applications, being visually oriented, easily recover from delays. Employees at this company, as with employees in most companies, were accustomed to seeing that hourglass on their screen.

"Ah, the system's just thinking."

"Network's a bit slow today."

What was actually happening at this company was that its spanning-tree algorithm on the network was resetting itself every 30 minutes or so. This meant that approximately every half-hour, the network, for the most part, went dumb, and had to relearn everything, such as which segments users were located on. During this time, packets were delayed and sometimes dropped, and this caused retransmissions.

Packets floating around on the network, being retransmitted when others were dropped, eventually get resequenced and presented to the end user's workstation. So, the information eventually made it to the its destination. The result was sometimes a one- or two-second delay. Users became accustomed to this and no one complained.

Adding voice to this network was a recipe for disaster. Voice can tolerate only a certain latency, or level of delay. While the network was relearning and thereby causing delays in packet delivery, voice quality would have sounded, in a best-case scenario, like a terrible cell-phone connection. In a worst-case situation, calls would have been dropped because of the constant delays.

The network assessment conducted prior to installation of phones, however, caught this problem within the first couple of hours and prevented a huge catastrophe. Without a proper assessment, this company would have joined the ranks of many others that have tried IP telephony and thought the technology did not work.

The network assessment also uncovered the fact that an IP-addressing scheme was abandoned in midproject a year before. Additionally, the customer planned to pass dozens of compressed calls across a private WAN that had a 56 K committed information rate (CIR). This would have yielded results only slightly better than the WAN customer that was discussed earlier in this chapter.

These problems, and what has to be done to prevent or resolve them, is precisely why identification of applications is so critical to the success of an IPT deployment. Companies who want to realize the full potential of their IPT environment will do more than use the network for voice traffic—they will also deploy applications. Identifying those applications, and their resource requirements, is an important part of the assessment process. Applications will be the key business driver behind IPT deployment. To the extent that applications are not part of a company's convergence plans, this is going to seem like an awful lot of work to do something that theyalready do—make phone calls. So, it has to be more than just phone calls.

# Planning an IP Telephony Pilot

An IP telephony pilot is actually a great idea—if it is conducted for the right reason. Often, companies conduct IPT pilots to see if the technology works. These companies are asking the wrong question. They'll get the right answer, but not to the right question.

The question, again, should not be: Does this technology work?

The technology works just fine. The question should be: "Will this technology work on my network, with my voice requirements?"

This is what companies should and could be piloting. Too often, companies take 10–20 phones and put them in their IS department and isolate them on a switch or two, and place calls between phones. It works beautifully—but it is working so flawlessly because they are testing an isolated environment. There's no data traffic on those segments to simulate a real environment.

Some companies take it to the next step, and place 20 or so phones out on their actual network. Even here, particularly if these phones are spread across multiple segments, problems are going to be masked.

Another category, unfortunately growing in number, considers a pilot of the technology placing 100 or so phones out on their network and watching what happens. Actually, what happens is often predictable. Network issues that are masked by the fact that data can tolerate delays and latency are exposed by the fact that voice cannot. The company comes to the incorrect conclusion that IP telephony is not ready yet.

More companies, however, are taking the opportunity to not only put IP phones in front of their users, but while these 10–20 users are testing the technology, the company is in the midst of conducting readiness assessments. They are also learning about their current voice and data networks, and the impact of bringing these two networks together. These companies learn enough to develop a comprehensive project plan—one that anticipates obstacles and develops an action plan to eliminate them (as further discussed in the final chapter of this book). These companies, without exception, put themselves in a great position for success with their IP telephony deployments.

The main lesson I have learned from working with hundreds of IP telephony customers, is this: Good proactive planning takes time, but it is worth it. This is not to say that companies who plan properly don't run into problems, but most of the problems they encounter are predicted during an assessment. The integration issues that they face are not surprises. They have established a baseline for performance and, therefore, have a starting point if they encounter problems.

The key is to remember that every network is different. All customers have their own voice tendencies, and every customer has a network that has its own issues—without exception. So, a white paper might prepare you for what *could* go wrong, but a VRA can tell you what *will* go wrong. That is a critical difference.

Believe it or not, I found the greatest analogy and testimonial for network assessment at a racecar track. A few years ago, the Texas Motor Speedway (TMS) was built between Dallas and Ft. Worth in Texas. This track initially opened with NASCAR (stock car) races. The initial races for these cars (and trucks) went off without a hitch.

A couple of years later, however, the faster CART (Indy-style) racers came for their inaugural race at TMS. The race had to be cancelled. During time trials, some of the drivers were experiencing dizziness and a couple actually reported blacking out in the turns. As it turned out, the banking degree in the turns was too steep for these cars—although it posed no problems to the cars from NASCAR.

In other words, the CART racers, which go faster than NASCAR vehicles, could not run on the infrastructure of this track, even though the NASCAR racers had no problems. Furthermore, although these same CART racers could not run at TMS, they had no problems running at other tracks including Indianapolis and Michigan tracks. The racing technology worked well on some tracks, but not on others. Enhancements made at TMS fixed the problem, and people enjoy the races every year now. Yet, the analogy holds — the track, like the network, provides the foundation. Changes weren't made to the cars to make them able to race, but rather to the track. Similarly, changes are made to the network to accommodate voice and new phones and applications.

# Common Misconceptions

Obtaining brand-new equipment/components is nice — but the design in how these technologies are deployed is just as critical. Putting a new router in place does nothing if that router doesn't have the capability to handle thousands of voice calls, if that is your current volume of PBX traffic.

New technology in the network is great if that technology has been designed and selected with convergence in mind. Also, replacing the infrastructure, even if it is a nice idea, lengthens the ROI timeframe. These factors should be considered when looking at new technology. A VRA, for example, might expose that a couple of edge routers need replacing — but not the entire infrastructure. The following section reviews some of the common misconceptions about IPT deployment.

## I Have Plenty of Bandwidth

A company's belief that its bandwidth is sufficient is probably the most common — and most dangerous — misconception heard from potential convergence companies. More than anything else, companies assume that because voice only uses 64 K of bandwidth and they have, at a minimum, 100 Mbps of bandwidth, bandwidth isn't going to be an issue.

As previously stated, this isn't a case of enough bandwidth, but how the bandwidth is shared. Remember, in the PBX world, bandwidth isn't an issue—everyone is guaranteed their slice. No matter what else is going on in the PBX or on the network, when I get my bandwidth from the PBX, nothing can affect it. This is not the case in the data world, where packets are resequenced and retransmitted while people share network resources. So although the IP network has plenty of bandwidth, it is not guaranteed bandwidth. That is the difference.

Clearly, the one area where bandwidth is an issue is on the WAN. Here, the bandwidth is generally much more finite, and only a certain number of voice and data sessions are supported for a fixed bandwidth—hence, proper planning and alternate routing is a must.

## I Don't Need QoS

Many customers don't turn on QoS for a variety of reasons and, often, these reasons are valid. Some customers decide to run parallel voice and data networks. In other words, they use the IP components such as Ethernet switches for connectivity, but they isolate voice Ethernet switches from data Ethernet switches. QoS is less of a requirement in these cases.

Generally speaking, maintaining proper QoS is a good idea any time a company is running fully converged applications and users on the same network, particularly where voice, video, and data are all being used. Furthermore, voice does not always take priority. Key video sessions, financial transactions, and daily updates often require priority on the network as well.

## It's Only Voice—Just More Bits and Bytes

Thankfully, it is now becoming rare for customers to trivialize the new technology. Most customers today understand that voice is different from data. It reacts differently to stimulus—positive and negative—and its users have an entirely different opinion of what high availability means.

## My Partner Knows Data—Voice Can't Be All That Difficult

The fact that many manufacturers are now tightening their requirements for the partners to sell, install, and support this technology speaks to the fact that these manufacturers have learned that both competencies are required to deal with this new technology. Although an in-depth understanding of data and IP technologies is necessary, a detailed understanding of voice, and experience with the expectations of phone users is just as important.

Consider the medical profession. Say you have a child who has a cold. You're not sure if it is something more, so you decide to take your child to the doctor. Most parents take their child to a pediatrician because this is a doctor who specializes in children's medicine. This doctor knows children's diseases and children's tendencies.

However, if it is determined that the child has a heart problem and surgery is required, the parents would not want the pediatrician to perform heart surgery. No, in this case, the parents would select someone who is an expert in dealing with heart problems—a heart specialist, or cardiologist. If possible, the parents would like to have a doctor who specializes in children's heart problems, a pediatric cardiologist.

In the medical profession, numerous disciplines and specialties exist. A patient might require care in many of these specialties throughout the course of a lifetime and would want to have access to the right skills for the given situation. So it is with IP telephony.

IP telephony requires partners who possess both data and voice skills. More specifically, it requires a partner who not only brings data skills, but specifically, IP configuration skills, unified messaging skills, quality of service skills, HTML/Java/XML skills. From a voice perspective, companies want partners with dial plan skills, alternate routing skills, messaging skills, TAPI skills. At any time, any and all these skill sets might come into play, and so companies need to ensure that they are partnering with organizations that have these competencies.

# Seven Steps to a Successful IP Telephony Experience

There are seven steps to convergence success. These are seven common traits, or elements, that I've seen in each case where a customer has had a successful IPT deployment. Some of these steps might appear to be simple common sense.

## Step 1: Identify Your Desired State

The first step is to have an objective. Companies who have had success with IP telephony can complete the following sentence:

We deployed IP telephony in order to _____.

As with any project, success begins with identifying the goal. People don't jump in the car with packed bags and the kids in the backseat and just start driving until they decide where they're going for vacation. They make plans, and the plans start with identifying the destination. So it is with convergence. The following is a list of possible objectives:

- For hotels, the goal might be a new application environment that enhances the customer experience when they stay at the hotel.

- For schools, it might be creating a safer, more secure environment for their students, or possibly enhancing the parent-teacher communications.

- For hospitals, it might be creating a flexible, innovative environment that attracts and retains the best doctors and nurses in the area.

- For a retail organization, it might be enhancing the payroll and time-reporting process to control and contain overtime expenses.

Finally, it might be as simple as an organization saying they want to reduce their budget across the board by 10 percent.

These are just examples of good objectives. Customers who have deployed IPT successfully have been able to achieve objectives such as these. There is no right or wrong goal—just have one, and make that the focus of the convergence journey.

## Step 2: Identify the Measurements for Success

This is a key element. What metrics will you use in order to measure, or assess, whether or not this was a successful journey? It's the roadmap for the journey. The metrics are those signposts or those landmarks that ensure you are on the right path.

In a review of the objectives previously listed, it is possible to identify a sampling of potential metrics:

- For hotels, if the goal is a new application environment that enhances the customer experience when they stay at the hotel, the metric could be customer satisfaction scores obtained from customers who use the new applications in a test environment.

- For schools, if the goal is to create a safer, more secure environment for students, the metric could be the development of an application that ties the school network in with the local police department, enabling alerts to be processed at the touch of a button. Alternatively, for the school whose goal is to enhance parent-teacher communications, it could be results of parental usage for a new messaging or interactive application accessing grades and interacting with teachers.

- For hospitals whose goal is to create a flexible, innovative environment that attracts and retains the best doctors and nurses in the area, the results of employee surveys of doctors and nurses is a good metric.

- For a retail organization, the goal is to enhance the payroll and time-reporting process to control and contain overtime expenses. The metric is simply the tracking of overtime paid for a period of time after the roll-out of a convergence application.

For the generic organization looking to reduce budget across the board by 10 percent, the metric is easy. Did they accomplish the goal?

Metrics are critical, as they remove the subjectivity and ambiguity from the process. They demand accountability and force organizations to set an objective in the first place.

## Step 3: Identify the Obstacles

As previously noted in this chapter, a number of obstacles can raise their heads to prevent a successful deployment. Furthermore, assessments can be performed to anticipate and predict certain obstacles, or gaps. Identifying these gaps and their causes, and developing action plans to eliminate them, is paramount to the success of the project.

For example, in the anecdote about the company that conducted a VRA *after* it had already deployed IPT and ran into problems, the VRA identified a router that was running at close to 90 percent utilization. If this company had decided to conduct the VRA *before* the installation, it would have known that its core router would not be able to handle the additional load associated with voice sessions, and the problem of dropped calls and one-way audio would have been avoided.

The gap, therefore, was the router's utilization levels. The symptom of the gap, seen afterwards, was dropped calls and one-way audio. The cause of the high utilization was the fact that this was a low-capacity router being stressed by existing applications. Identifying potential gaps or obstacles greatly lessens (if not eliminates) the pain that can be associated with convergence deployments. Whatever the root cause, obstacles must be anticipated and addressed for a convergence project to achieve success.

## Step 4: Develop Action Plans to Eliminate Obstacles

After the gaps are identified, a detailed action plan to eliminate the gaps is required. This is a critical step, because all too often companies develop action plans that contain activities that sound logical, and appear beneficial—but have absolutely no impact on obstacles or gaps. It is important to be ruthless in your management technique to ensure that no additional activities that do not address known obstacles or gaps are added.

In the previous example, where an overutilized router was identified as the gap, the action taken was to upgrade the router, and to reconfigure the QoS parameters in the new router. Both actions eliminated gaps, and with the gaps eliminated, so too were the symptoms—namely, dropped calls and one-way audio sessions.

## Step 5: Celebrate Your Achievements

The importance of this element cannot be stressed enough. It has been demonstrated that many successful organizations went through an incremental deployment as a means of embracing convergence. As a reminder, an incremental deployment allows a company to identify a set number of employees, or departments, and incrementally migrate them from their PBX to the IP telephony solution. In doing so, the company can set short-term goals, develop applications to achieve the goals, and manage the gaps and obstacles more effectively.

As soon as a department or group of employees has successfully been transitioned, and a newly developed application has proven successful, it is important to celebrate this win for the company. This incredible achievement sets the stage (and lays the emotional and political foundation) for the remaining phases of the deployment.

It is helpful to remember that people are averse to change—so any positive achievements that are a result of the project should be proactively and publicly celebrated by the organization.

Nothing helps people accept change faster than when they become aware of how change actually succeeded in doing something positive for the company, or the department, or the team. Celebrate your victories publicly—and often.

## Step 6: Be Committed, Not Curious

The most important advice I give to potential customers is that IP telephony is not something to dabble with. A company has to commit to convergence. Companies that have deployed IPT successfully have identified a champion, someone internally in the organization who, because of the promise of IPT, was willing to step out, take a risk, and let the accountability fall on his shoulders. Clearly, the risk is not all theirs, and the risk is greatly mitigated by careful planning, including network assessments to identify potential obstacles. Yet the fact remains that convergence is all about change, and change can be considered risky.

Because most IP networks were not originally designed and configured with desktop voice transmissions in mind, it is logical to assume that companies that migrate their voice communications to their IP networks are going to run into issues. This is simply because their existing networks were not designed to handle this type of traffic. That is no reason to throw in the towel, so to speak, and terminate the IPT migration project. The migration becomes easier when potential issues are identified up front, but this requires a commitment from your organization.

| NOTE | Don't wonder whether you might have problems during an IP telephony migration. Assume that obstacles will arise, then identify them proactively, and eliminate them with company initiatives. |
|------|------|

Companies that commit to convergence set a goal for the organization, put metrics in place, create a detailed plan that anticipates gaps and obstacles, develope action plans to eliminate the gaps, and manage the process to a successful conclusion.

## Step 7: Select the Right Partner

Selecting the right partner can mean the difference between successfully deploying an enterprise-wide solution that radically changes a company for the better—or just installing technology in silos within an organization, compounding existing problems by adding yet another barrier between teams and departments.

| NOTE | The right partner can help overcome product deficiencies and help identify potential gaps. |
|------|------|

A partner who understands and has experience with both voice and data can help a company with 2500 users migrate those users from their PBX technologies to IP telephony at a gradual pace that is right for the company. The right partner is able to do this because they know how to allow the new technologies to coexist with the old. However, a partner who only understands voice, or only understands data, might rush the project to a rapid conclusion because they don't have the competency to allow the technologies to work together for lengthy periods of time.

A company that has multiple voice-mail platforms is going to require someone who understands messaging. That same company might have a wireless/mobility strategy in place that requires a transition to 802.11 technologies. The right partner will have both skills.

In the end, following these seven steps can greatly impact a company's desires to move towards a network deployment that enables new technologies, new applications, and new benefits for an organization.

# CHAPTER 8

# LOOKING AHEAD

Late in 1999, during a Cisco sponsored road show designed to help customers better understand IP telephony, Ken Bywaters, senior development manager for Berbee, told the following story:

In the early 1900s, families were accustomed to getting their morning milk delivery. A few times during the week, Harry, the local milkman would come by, riding in his carriage pulled by his trusty horse. House to house he went, delivering bottles of milk to familiar faces.

Day after day, he followed his familiar route, and customers no doubt grew accustomed to the familiar clip clop as the hooves of the horse announced the arrival of their milk delivery.

One day, however, as Harry sat dozing in his rocking chair in the family den by the warm fireplace, he was awakened by a knock at the door. He opened the door and was warmly greeted by a salesman.

As it turns out, this salesman was trying to sell him a new piece of technology that would enable him to make his deliveries faster—perhaps cutting a couple of hours off his workday, giving him back more free time.

What was this new technology? The milk truck.

Harry, of course, looked at the salesman as though he had just fallen off a horse (no pun intended).

"A what?" Harry asked.

The salesman took Harry outside and showed him the new marvel: an automobile. An automated horse, if you will—one that doesn't eat, doesn't sleep, doesn't need a special barn, and one that can run much faster.

"Think about it, Harry" the salesman went on. "A new way to deliver milk faster. You can get out and get back home so fast. Won't Gina be happy to see you home earlier? Think of the extra time you can spend with the kids."

"But I like my horse," replied Harry.

Back and forth they went, the salesman trying to show Harry the benefits of something new, and Harry wondering why in the world he would discard his horse. His horse was proven, faithful, and loyal. His horse was his friend. He and his horse had a system in place and his horse already knew the route. Life was easy.

"But life can be better," the salesman said.

"I don't need life to be better," Harry insisted. "There's nothing wrong with my horse. I don't need any fancy auto-mo-bile."

There was lots of laughter (admittedly, self-conscious laughter) in the audience when Ken told this story. Many people saw themselves in this story. The horse was their PBX. The milk truck was IP telephony.

"My PBX works just fine."

"You want me to run voice on my IP network? Are you crazy?"

"I like things the way they are."

Wisely, Ken let everyone off the hook with his punchline:

"Of course, ladies and gentlemen, we all know how this story turned out. We ended up buying milk trucks and eating our horses."

Still, the point was made—looking back, change not only seems easy, but necessary. For example, does anyone long for the days before PCs when workers depended totally on a large, dumb terminal? Does anyone truly miss rotary phones?

"There's nothing wrong with my telephone. I can dial numbers easily, thank you very much. I don't need this touch-tone stuff."

Changes in this industry are happening before our eyes, both in terms of technical functionality and customer acceptance. Companies considering this technology often find themselves asking long-range, strategic questions about IP telephony:

- Where is this technology going?
- What kind of applications will we see two or three years from now?
- How quickly are new phones going to hit the market?
- Will my investment today be obsolete in a year?

Companies want to know for certain that they are making the right decision, and they want to know what to expect so they can plan appropriately.

This book has looked at what is happening today in the IP telephony market. This final chapter takes a forward look at what can be expected in the near future for IPT. The primary areas of this discussion center on new types of clients (devices), new applications, and improved management. This chapter also explores the changing market for IP telephony.

# Clients

The development of new clients, or new devices, is an area of both excitement and concern for potential buyers of IP telephony. On the one hand, continuous emergence of new phones and devices only reaffirms this technology, the market, and the manufacturers who participate in the market. On the other hand, it does cause reluctance to go out and buy hundreds or thousands of new phones today, knowing that a radically different type of phone is likely to become available within a year or less.

New IP phones can be realistically expected to appear at the same rate that new cell phone technologies now come to market.

Figure 8-1 depicts a new type of convergence client that was introduced at the 2003 Cisco IP Telephony Users Group meeting in Dallas, Texas. This new client, dubbed a *virtual interactive agent* by its developers at Norstan CDG, is a radical departure from the early softphones of the 1990s.

***Figure 8-1*** *PC-Based Virtual Interactive Agent*

The virtual interactive agent looks nothing like a phone. This is by design, so as not to restrict the end users' view of the technology. Running on the end user's laptop or desktop device, this client provides desktop-to-desktop voice, video, and instant messaging sessions all across the corporate IP network. From a single application, users can communicate in the manner they see best, for that particular moment.

The virtual interactive agent is voice activated and provides *extended messaging*; that is, the ability to record messages and extend delivery of those messages, via e-mail, to users beyond the corporate voice-messaging network. Finally, it provides an interactive *help entity,* which is a visual representation of a help agent to walk the user through features and capabilities.

As public wireless locations become more prevalent, Wi-Fi has emerged as a phenomenon. Wireless laptop users are often seen in public spots not only accessing the web and their corporate network (via VPN), but using a client to stay connected from a voice and video perspective, to their corporate environment if they so choose. In fact, wherever an end user can access a high-speed Internet connection and VPN into his corporate network, this type of client enables them to place and receive voice and video calls. It also handles instant-messaging sessions using his corporate IM standard, whether they are at home, in a hotel, or in a public setting.

Extend this capability to the PDA, and now you have a viable alternative to the cell phone. More often, cell phones are attempting to become data devices; they browse the web, take digital pictures, shoot video clips, send text messages, and play games. Yet they do this over the cellular network, with its inherent problems of coverage. A Wi-Fi user, however, armed with the proper tools, has a device that was designed at the foundation to handle these types of sessions (a PDA or laptop), and an IP telephony soft client adds the voice and video communications in a cost-effective manner.

# Applications

New IP phones that support color displays and touch-screen capabilities are already available from Cisco Systems. Video support is not that far behind. The phone is going to start to operate like a PC. Issuing commands and launching telephony applications via icons as opposed to the telephone dial pad will become commonplace. The real interest, however, is beginning to center around voice activation.

## Voice Activation

Voice-activated applications are probably the most eagerly awaited benefit of IP telephony from the perspective of future implementations. Today, most implementations of speech recognition technologies have focused on the call center, replacing caller keystrokes with caller voice commands. This has been a good start to prove the technology. However, finding specialized applications, aimed at specific industry business processes, that benefit from voice-activated commands will be a key focal point for integrators in the coming years.

In certain scenarios, the ability to "speak" to an application without using a keypad or keyboard can be a critical productivity aid. A nurse making rounds on the hospital floor, or a dock worker handling products are two examples where the ability to issue voice commands to an application that handles voice, data, or video can be beneficial. Voice-activated applications can greatly enhance businesses where dial pad or keyboard keystrokes are the only option today.

For example, instead of the user having to remember to press 7 and 3 to replay a message, he or she could simply say the word "replay." Instead of having to remember various numeric commands, the user could issue voice commands; and the voice user interface (VUI), will be multilingual to enable a global implementation for large, worldwide enterprises.

It is easy to imagine these applications migrating to a more data-centric implementation. IP telephony, for example, could completely redefine distance learning in primary and secondary schools (K–12).

In 1995, my family and I were in a serious car accident. My oldest daughter, Tylen, then 12 years old, took the brunt of the accident, when the seat belt sliced into her abdomen. She spent well over a month in the hospital, with teachers visiting after school to keep her up to date academically. In addition, one of my sons, Alex, spent two weeks in the hospital with a broken femur bone, then spent the next month at home in bed, basically immobile with screws and pins in his leg. He, too, fell far behind in his schoolwork, because he had to depend on friends bringing his classwork and an occasional visit from a teacher.

IP telephony will enable teachers to take advantage of established wireless cable-modem and DSL technologies to produce a virtual classroom from the hospital bed. Soon, PC-based softphone/soft-client capabilities with embedded video support will allow a student patient to establish a VPN connection with his or her school. This connection will enable the student to see and hear everything going on in the classroom, as well as ask questions and fully interact with teachers and classmates—all from a laptop provided by the school.

Students who are immobilized will be able to issue voice commands to control the application, video windows, and interactive capabilities. This will all be accomplished without a physical phone at the hospital bed. A headset or earpiece connected to the wireless laptop in the room will accommodate their voice and video requirements. The foundation for this technology is already visible at various locations today, including airports, hotel lobbies, and Starbucks coffee shops.

In addition, the entire school day, or portions thereof, can be recorded and then sent as a streaming file to the student at a later time, for those occasions when hospital procedures prevent the student patient from attending in real time. This useful implementation of technology could actually help keep the student caught up, yet does not require the teacher(s) to put in additional hours (and drive time) for their efforts.

## Customized Solutions

Companies are now realizing that the real power of IP telephony lies not in the new clients, but in how well they integrate these new clients into their business processes. The client—whether an IP phone or a soft client running on a laptop, wireless tablet, or PDA—becomes the foundation on which effective applications will be created, and these applications will be created based on business need.

Consider the Emergency Alert System (EAS), which was established by the Federal Communications Commission (FCC) for the United States in November of 1994. The EAS replaced the Emergency Broadcast System, which was designed as a means to warn the public about emergency situations. EAS uses digital technology to communicate warning messages for weather hazards (such as tornadoes, flash floods, and hurricanes), as well as other situations, to the public. Through the integration efforts of convergence applications integrator AAC Associates, Inc., these alerts can now be delivered audibly and visually to Cisco IP phones, as shown in Figure 8-2. This is an example of an application customized to a specific requirement—enhanced notification for the Emergency Alert System.

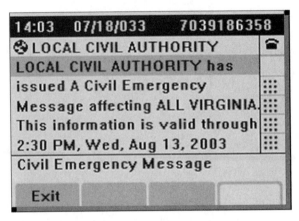

*Figure 8-2* Integration of EAS with IP Phones

Other warning scenarios, such as the Amber Alert created in 1996 in the United States to track and monitor child kidnappings, are also integrated into IP telephony solutions and delivered to IP phones. Figure 8-3 shows a sample screen, again delivered by AAC Associates, which tracks progress during an Amber Alert situation and communicates status to IP phones. This is especially useful for secondary schools and/or local government agencies that have deployed IP telephony, because it gives yet another means of quickly communicating vital information. This is an example of customization aimed at a specific requirement.

*Figure 8-3* Integration of Amber Alerts with IP Phones

The potential is endless. IP telephony applications are expected to touch virtually every industry in the coming years:

- **Gas stations**—Expect price changes and alerts to drive this market, with interactive soft clients enhancing communications between station employees and corporate offices.

- **Shopping malls and department stores**—Customers inquiring about merchandise in other store branches won't be subject to the multiple phone calls to other stores that retail stores put them through today. An IPT application will quickly identify the nearest store with the requested merchandise, and automatically place a call to that store requesting them to place the merchandise on hold.

- **Pharmacy applications**—A patient who places a prescription order (or a refill order) will automatically generate an audible and visual alert on an IP phone in the pharmacy, notifying them of an incoming prescription request. In this way, the prescription is more likely to be filled by the time the patient gets to the pharmacy, thereby enhancing customer satisfaction.

- **Customer support centers** will adopt virtual interactive agents, enabling their customers to establish video sessions with support personnel over a high-speed Internet connection. This will not only enhance the customer experience, but enable the company itself to reduce the number of toll-free trunks coming into its call centers, which reduces a key recurring cost for call center organizations.

- **Banks and financial institutions** will be able to better support their customers, as advanced IP telephony applications integrated with their back-end databases assess market conditions throughout the day, and immediately develop contact lists of customers the broker should call, based on real-time market activity.

- **Local government organizations** will link to their public school networks, enabling rapid alerting capabilities to IP phones on desktops, or even in police cars on the street equipped with wireless technologies.

- **Airlines**—Many airlines today are experimenting with airborne Internet access, and as soon as this is accomplished, in-flight voice and video calls are just an application and click away. This will also drive additional revenue for the airlines.

Virtually every industry will adopt this technology in large numbers in the coming years, as their existing PBXs are written off the books, and IP telephony applications become more prevalent. The key, again, lies in the manufacturer, or partners' ability to have a different type of discussion with the companies they serve. This discussion must go beyond telephone features and focus on business initiatives and business process.

# Managing Convergence

The final, uncharted waters for applications will focus on management and administration. Clearly, the opportunity exists to streamline multiple platforms and organizations into a single entity that can manage the entire enterprise network: voice, data, video, and collaboration. The question is how to deploy new management techniques and processes that take advantage of a single network.

We can expect to see new applications, or applets, at the desktop level to enable companies to self-manage and monitor devices/clients on the network, regardless of their use. Voice devices (phones) will be managed by the same platform that can handle data devices (PCs). New applications will focus on being more proactive in identifying potential problems, and alerting the right people — both within the organization and potentially within that company's support partner organization.

Chapter 7, "Watch That First Step," explained the need to assess the network environment prior to deploying IP telephony. It follows that it also makes sense to conduct such assessments periodically as companies begin to add additional users and new applications that will generate additional traffic on the network.

# Session Initiation Protocol

No discussion about IP telephony is complete without covering the Session Initiation Protocol (SIP). SIP is a signaling protocol used to establish sessions in an IP network. A *session* can be something as complex as a collaborative voice/video/data conversation, or something as simple as a phone call. The IPT market has adopted SIP as the protocol of choice for long-term strategic direction. As of this writing, SIP remains a draft from the Internet Engineering Task Force, which is the organization responsible for developing and administering the methodology driving Internet communications. To this extent, SIP is still evolving as the IPT market matures.

SIP is important because it is simple and straightforward, and it is designed to do one thing: establish/set up sessions. SIP doesn't need to know all the variant details of a session—it just establishes the session, modifies the session, or releases the session.

SIP inherently uses other existing protocols, which means that it does not try to do everything. SIP has a role and it is designed to play that role specifically. So, by working with other protocols and not forcing additional functionality into SIP itself, this is a protocol that scales extremely well. Being modeled after HTTP and SMTP, SIP is compatible with other web-based applications.

The ability to establish these sessions enables a myriad of innovative capabilities or services. Capabilities such as web page click-to-dial, instant messaging with buddy lists, and video-embedded text are examples of functionality SIP can be expected to provide cost-effectively to the market.

The real win for companies, however, is going to be choice. That is the reason for discussing SIP in lieu of other potential protocols. Adherence to the SIP standard by manufacturers will mean a new level of choice for organizations when it comes to telephony devices. It will enable a company to deploy any number of clients it chooses from any manufacturer that has adopted SIP, knowing full well that the clients will work properly and can be managed from the same platform.

Consider a typical IP network with infrastructure equipment such as switches and routers that can be implemented from a number of manufacturers. In your own network, you might see any number of clients, ranging from IBM personal computers, to Dell servers, to Toshiba laptops—all from different manufacturers running on the same network. This is the promise of SIP. Upon being ratified by the standards bodies, SIP promises a similar environment where companies have a wider range of choices for their desktop IP telephony devices, regardless of which manufacturers' product was selected for call-control.

Finally, SIP is expected to create a host of new companies that can provide applications, devices (clients), and management capabilities without regard to manufacturer, which can benefit the entire market.

# An Evolving Market/An Emerging Market/ Increased Acceptance

Looking toward the future, things look bright for the IP telephony industry. Right or wrong, many companies view the fact that PBX manufacturers are finally stepping into this industry in a significant way as a validation of sorts—even if they decide to move forward with a non-Nortel or non-Avaya deployment. Just the fact that these manufacturers believe the market to be viable is enough for many companies to justify any purchase of IPT technologies.

IP telephony is the strategic direction that companies are embracing when it comes to telecommunications. According to numbers from InfoTech, an independent research organization that has been tracking the IPT market since its inception, a total of just over 1.8 million combined PBX/IPT lines shipped in the fourth quarter of 2002, running from October 1 through December 31. Of these 1.8 million ports, roughly 571,000 were IP telephony ports. Therefore, during the last three months of 2002, approximately 31 percent, or almost one third of all lines shipped, were IP telephony.

This is significant for two reasons. First, it is a continuing trend, and a significant year-over-year growth for this industry. Just two years ago, the number of IP telephony ports shipped as a percentage of all shipments was in the single digits. Second, this is significant because in 2003, a number of people still believe that IPT is in the early adopter phase.

I still hear customers say they "don't want to be the first" to deploy this technology. With one third of all shipments falling under the IPT category, it is safe to say that the train has left the station, so to speak. This technology has progressed beyond the early adopter phase and is now being embraced by companies both large and small, across all industries.

Continual consolidation is expected to be seen in the market. No doubt, Norstan's acquisition of NetCom Systems for application development in early 2003 will not be the last acquisition of this type. Partnerships in the future are going to be developed between strange bedfellows. For potential customers, it is difficult to find a partner that understands voice, data, video, security, network services, and application development. Therefore, alliances between partners is going to be the norm, with occasional acquisitions to formalize relationships.

# Final Thoughts

The IP telephony market has come a long way since my early lunch meeting with Richard Platt and David Tucker. An entire industry has emerged and is in the process of fully maturing, with additional IP clients being developed and deployed almost quarterly by a host of different manufacturers. It is enabling a multitude of new applications, most of which had not been imagined prior to the IPT deployment. It is introducing a new type of ROI—a new model for measuring total cost of ownership. Finally, it is bringing a new level of intelligence to the device which is arguably the most important in the enterprise—the telephone.

Where the technology goes from here is limited only by the imagination. Telephones and PCs are going to undergo a metamorphosis. A gradual blending of capabilities is underway so that, ultimately, a single, integrated device will be the workstation of choice for the business worker both at the desktop and while on the move. It will be cost-effective as well as functionally superior to its predecessors.

Ultimately, this new functionality will be driven by cost-containment opportunities. As the latter half of this decade approaches, company financial officers are going to question the necessity for maintaining one workstation at the desk for voice, and another for data, as well as maintaining separate voice and data networks, and departments to support them. Finances will drive the decision, and end users will benefit from the new functionality provided.

The promise of convergence is the intelligent blending of disparate capabilities to provide added value at a reduced cost. This movement is underway, and quickly growing. Cisco Systems and other network-savvy companies have laid the foundation. The movement is accelerating as traditional PBX leaders such as Nortel gain acceptance with their IP telephony offerings. It will finally reach its full potential with the proliferation and adoption of industry protocols, such as SIP, as a standards-based foundation for new clients and applications by suppliers and developers who, currently, have been held out of the market by the proprietary nature of telecommunications offerings.

Only time will tell how quickly this metamorphosis might progress. However, the days of an intelligent, rapidly evolving data device sitting next to a static, nonintelligent voice device, with separate wireless devices independently acquired by end users are numbered. This is an expensive model, one that is only now being challenged, and one that will go the way of other great inventions that have been left behind by the advance of new technology.

In considering what can be expected in the future, it is important to remember what has been learned from history. Who among us saw color, web-surfing, or instant-messaging cell phones—even five years ago? Who among us foresaw the Internet becoming what it has evolved into? The key applications that are truly going to impact the business world are, at this moment, in the minds of the customer who could benefit from them. This is both exciting and frustrating, depending on your point of view.

In 1980, the concept of an office without typewriters was absurd. The back closet room still had teletypes. Lanier and Wang word processors were in vogue. Companies had a data entry system, a separate departmental system, and a mainframe environment—multiple layers of cost. Today, with the exception of the mainframe still found in large organizations, each of these technologies previously mentioned, although incredibly innovative and valuable in their time, are distant memories. The college graduates that businesses will depend on in the coming decade have likely not seen any of those technologies, and they are far more apt to demand new technologies.

As a colleague of mine once commented, "We are rapidly coming to the day where the most advanced and impressive technology used by young people entering the work environment will no longer be the PlayStation or XBox, but rather the technology they use at their business desktop."

That, more than anything else, defines the need for convergence in business today.

# INDEX

K-12 education, 84–88
retail business, 91–93
security applications, 96–97
reliance on vender support, 78
reliance on vital few initiatives, 73
**IP networks, VoIP gateways, 7–8**
**IP phones, 9**
evolution of, 64–65
**IP-Rail, 58**
**IPT pilot, planning, 139–141**

# K–L

**K-12 education, identifying business needs, 84–88**

**lack of bandwidth availability, 131–132**
**line cards, 20**
**line-side connectivity, 22**
**linking user profiles, 38**
**lost calls, 135**

# M

**maintenance costs of IPT deployment, 110, 112**
**management and administration applications, 160**
**maximizing ROI, 101**
administration costs, 110
in banking and finance industry, 113
in retail deployment, 114–116
in secondary education deployment, 113–114
maintenance costs, 110–112
network costs, 102–103
convergence deployments, 104, 107–108
**migrating to IPT**
incremental deployments, 66–70
training, 45–48

**misconceptions of IPT**
availability of bandwidth, 141
necessity of QoS, 142
necessity of voice expertise, 143
**monitoring IPT, user alerts, 27–28, 157–159**

# N–O

**necessity of QoS, misconceptions, 142**
**NetCom Systems, IP-Rail, 57**
**network switches, 21**

**obstacles to convergence, 14–15**
**one-way audio, 134**
**open standard IPT architecture, 52**

# P

**paging, 29**
**PBX environment, 19**
components, 20
consolidation with IPT, 162
features sets, 34–35
forced authorization codes, 39–44
linking user profiles, 38
time-of-day ringing, 37
paging, 29
proprietary nature of, 26
replicating on IPT infrastructure, 24–25
training new IPT users, 35–36
voice/data integration, disadvantages of
contention, 4
lack of industry standards, 6
slow line speeds, 6
**performance, VRA, 128–130**
**piloting an IPT deployment, 139–141**
**planning an IPT pilot, 139–141**